IMAGES
of America

KINDERHOOK

ON THE COVER: With an ongoing prosperity from agriculture, Kinderhook is known to be one of the oldest towns in New York State. (Courtesy of the Library of Congress.)

IMAGES of America
KINDERHOOK

Lisa LaMonica
Foreword by Bruce G. Hallenbeck

Copyright © 2019 by Lisa LaMonica
ISBN 978-1-4671-0360-2

Published by Arcadia Publishing
Charleston, South Carolina

Printed in the United States of America

Library of Congress Control Number: 2019931553

For all general information, please contact Arcadia Publishing:
Telephone 843-853-2070
Fax 843-853-0044
E-mail sales@arcadiapublishing.com
For customer service and orders:
Toll-Free 1-888-313-2665

Visit us on the Internet at www.arcadiapublishing.com

*This book is dedicated to the Mohicans, the original people
of Columbia County, whose story still fascinates me.*

Contents

Foreword		6
Acknowledgments		7
Introduction		8
1.	Early Kinderhook	9
2.	Martin Van Buren and Lindenwald	13
3.	Jesse Merwin, Ichabod Crane, and Washington Irving	31
4.	Architecture	49
5.	Notable Residents Past and Present	57
6.	Folklore and Local Lore	65
7.	A Mosaic of Kinderhook	75

Foreword

History and folklore often intertwine in Kinderhook; for example, Martin Van Buren, the eighth president of the United States, was born and is buried in Kinderhook, and he supposedly coined the term "OK," which, according to local historians, originally stood for "Old Kinderhook." And, needless to say, his presidential ghost reputedly haunts his old home of Lindenwold, which still stands just off Route 9H, not far from the original Ichabod Crane schoolhouse. Kinderhook is noted as one of the more haunted places in the Hudson Valley, which is saying quite a lot for an area inhabited by all manner of ghosts, ghouls, and things that go bump in the night. After all, Washington Irving's Headless Horseman rode through the Hudson Valley in pursuit of Ichabod Crane, just to name one of the most famous examples of Hudson Valley folklore.

I am happy to say that I have apparently contributed to Kinderhook's mysterious reputation. If one takes a tour through the vast hallways of the Internet, one can find a website called cryptidz.fandom.com, which features a page or two on the so-called Kinderhook Blob. At least, that's what I called it when I was a kid. The website entry, written by I know not whom, begins, "In 1960s New York, no fewer than six witnesses encountered a floating, mysterious blob-like creature that was so terrifying two armed men fled from it in terror. The story of this creature began in Kinderhook, New York. The first report, from 1962, comes from a 10-year-old boy (at the time) and his seven-year-old cousin. Chari. The rest are from people who happened to be in the woods several years after."

That 10-year-old boy was me, and he's still very much alive in my grownup body. And that was far from the last odd "creature" that apparently dwelled in Kinderhook; during the 1980s, a Sasquatch-like man-beast terrorized several residents of the old Dutch village. It was investigated by a television program called *PM Magazine*, who dubbed it "The Kinderhook Creature." LaMonica has written a wonderful book about Kinderhook and has compiled mountains of photographs and imagery of the quaint little town and its history and folklore. She has captured, beautifully, the history and folklore of the place, hopefully inspiring those who have never traveled its byways to come and visit, and to share Kinderhook's magic with its residents.

I hope you have a great time with this book. I did.

—Bruce G. Hallenbeck

Acknowledgments

Unless otherwise noted, all images appear courtesy of the Library of Congress.

Thank you to my son Patrick Robert Mason; my friends Tom D'Onofrio and John Craig; Ann Cooper of Columbia County Tourism; Jon Meredith; Jonathan Kruk; Tom Illari; Bruce Hallenbeck; and Shelby Mattice/The Bronck Museum.

Introduction

Kinderhook is known to be one of the oldest towns in New York State, and its significance to the nation's history and culture cannot be understated. One of America's presidents, Martin Van Buren, resided in Kinderhook. The Kinderhook connection to Washington Irving and the prominence of his "The Legend of Sleepy Hollow" is of significant literary importance; the story being considered one of the most important pieces of literature to shape a nation.

English explorer Henry Hudson is credited with "discovering" the Kinderhook area in September 1609; it was where his ship the *Half Moon* remained anchored for four days. His sailing party was welcomed by the Mohicans, or Mahicans, as referred to by the Dutch. The natives gave the newcomers Indian corn, pumpkins, and tobacco. Fortunately for readers, Hudson's clerk Robert Juet kept meticulous entries in a daily journal. He wrote, "We found very loving people and very old men and were well used." His journals document the people and customs found in Kinderhook's early history among its original inhabitants.

The center of everyone's attention was the group of children gathered on the shore who first witnessed Hudson and his ship approaching and reportedly raced to tell the elders what they saw. They must have thought it a great fish rising above the waters. For these children, the name *Kinderhoeck*, meaning "Children's Corner," was created. Kinderhook was settled before 1651 and established as a town in 1788 from a district previously created in 1772, but it lost substantial territory used to form part of the town of Chatham in 1775. Kinderhook was one of the original towns of Columbia County. The population now is quite different mainly due to the influx of New Yorkers during the 1980s. The main source of commerce in Kinderhook is farming—especially apples, closely followed by real estate. "During the 20th century, Kinderhook was an agricultural mecca. That hasn't changed dramatically, although the population has increased and become more diverse. It has always been an upscale area, and is probably even more so now," explains Kinderhook resident and author Bruce Hallenbeck.

Washington Irving was the first American literary figure to achieve vast international success from his work as well as being the first American to make his living completely from his writing. It is strongly believed that the tale of Ichabod Crane was written in Kinderhook and based on many of its residents whom Washington Irving befriended and lived among. He created a character, the Headless Horseman, that became a beloved and feared symbol not only in the United States but internationally as well, giving the Hudson Valley practically ownership over Halloween. To this day, the Headless Horseman is continually depicted in writing and film.

Kinderhook's stories of folklore, the Mohicans, Henry Hudson's discovery, and modern cultural happenings such as feature film production are still fascinating, worth telling and retelling so that they are not lost to time.

We owe a great deal to the Mohicans, and it is imperative to repeatedly tell their story and to honor them as the first inhabitants of Kinderhook.

These days, celebrated art galleries and restaurants, voted best in the county, attract visitors and locals. A population of 97 percent mostly white has not changed much over time. The Treasure Shop and the Old Dutch Inn were favorites in the 20th century; they are gone now. Shortly after their closings, Kinderhook's economy was sluggish for a time but has rebounded with the addition of more farm-to-table–style businesses.

One

EARLY KINDERHOOK

The first owner of the present site of Kinderhook village was Mohican chief Emikee, who also owned a portion of the flats toward Valatie. Valatie was a recurring meeting place of the Mohican tribe. *Packaquak*, meaning "meeting place" to them, was their name for Valatie.

As required by the Dutch in 1629 and later the English in 1664, it was necessary for an Indian owner or chief of the tribe to appear in person before Albany authorities testifying to being satisfied with the impending sale of land. It was the function of their head sachem, or peace chief, Eskuvius to negotiate peace, navigating treaties for their people and for others. The law regarding purchase and sale of land is referred to as "Lawes establisht by the Authority of His Majestees Letters patent granted to his Royall Highnes James Duke of Yorke and Albany" in Collier's *A History of Old Kinderhook from Aboriginal Days to the Present Time*.

Only after their terrible defeat by the Mohawks on Roger's Island in 1629 did the Mohicans consent to sale of their lands. In 1664, an Indian party (probably from Canada) had invaded and burned the Staats house in Stockport. In 1696, Captain Dubeau, his army, and Indians from Canada marched from Fort Orange to attack Kinderhook until Mohicans surprised and defeated them. It was also Mohicans, upon learning of Fort Orange's impending attack by French and their allies, who answered the call to arms defending the fort. James Fenimore Cooper's account of these events is chronicled in the book and film versions of *The Last of the Mohicans*.

The early Kinderhook District encompassed parts of Stockport, Valatie, Stuyvesant, Niverville, Chatham and Ghent, with all of Stuyvesant and part of Stockport being removed from Kinderhook in 1823. In 1772, Columbia County as it is now known was part of Albany County, with Kinderhook removed to its own district. In 1788, the Town of Kinderhook was defined; in 1838, the Village of Kinderhook was incorporated and defined.

Pictured is Edward Moran's c. 1898 painting of Henry Hudson entering New York Bay on September 11, 1609, with a Mohican family depicted watching from the shore in the foreground. According to journals kept at the time, Henry Hudson also entertained some of the Mohicans aboard his ship the *Half Moon*. Fur trading with the Mohicans would begin a year after Hudson's time at Kinderhook and his return to his homeland.

This 1909 image shows a replica of Henry Hudson's ship the *Half Moon*, reconstructed for the Hudson-Fulton Celebration, which took place from September 25 to October 9, 1909, in New York and New Jersey. The replica was a gift of the State Historical Society of Colorado in 1949 and marked the 300-year anniversary of his discovery of the river and the 100th anniversary of Robert Fulton's first steamship.

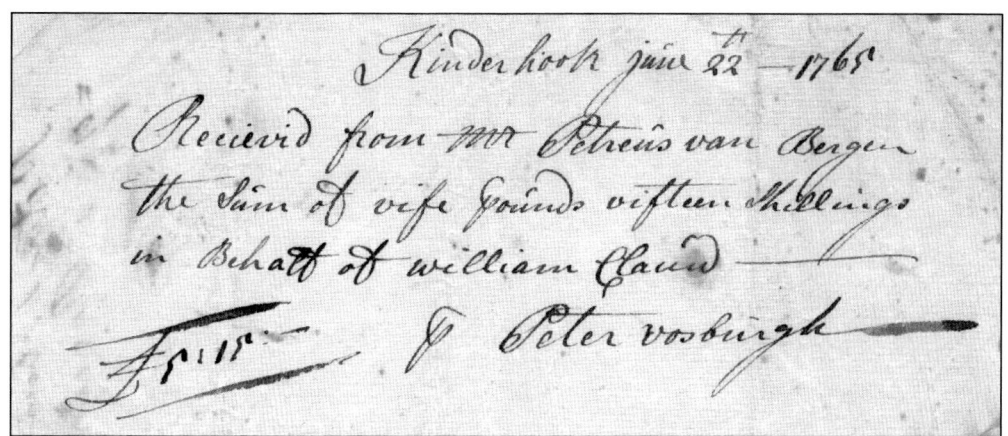

This Colonial-era document was signed by Peter Vosburgh in Kinderhook on June 22, 1765. It reads, "Received from Mr. Petreus Van Berger the sum of vife [five is spelled phonetically based on a Dutch accent] pounds, 15 shillings in behalf of William Claud. Peter Vosburgh." According to the records of the Dutch Church, the Vosburghs were among the first residents of Kinderhook in 1697. (Author's collection.)

Pictured is a map of Columbia County, New York, which was formed in 1786 and named for Christopher Columbus. Ancillary maps show towns surrounding Kinderhook, such as Austerlitz, Canaan Four Corners, Chatham, Chatham Four Corners, Claverack, Columbiaville and Stockport, Copake Flats, East Chatham, Hillsdale, Johnstown, Kinderhook, Lebanon Springs, Malden Bridge, Mellenville, North Chatham, Philmont, Spencertown, Stuyvesant Falls, Stuyvesant Landing, and Valatie.

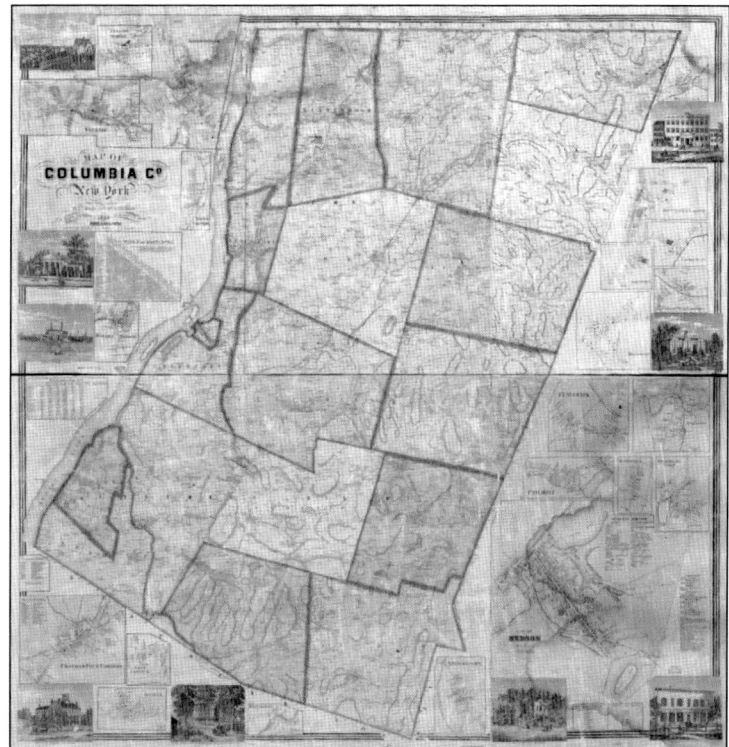

This image, called the *Last of the Mohicans*, was taken on November 17, 1920. The following quote by Edward Augustus Collier in his book *A History of Old Kinderhook from Aboriginal Days to the Present Time* refers to the Mohicans' perceptions of their treatment by foreigners: "The blood ran in streams into our fire and extinguished it so entirely that not one spark was left us whereby to kindle a new fire. The whites will not rest contented until they shall have destroyed the last of us, and made us disappear entirely from the face of the earth."

Henry Hudson's ship *Half Moon* is depicted anchored in the Hudson River, New York, in 1609, with Indian canoes approaching. The engraving is by S. Hollyer from September 2, 1909. Explorer Henry Hudson is credited with "discovering" Kinderhook in September 1609 when the *Half Moon* remained anchored in the area for four days. His sailing party was welcomed by the Mohicans. The natives gave food products and tobacco to the explorers.

Two
Martin Van Buren and Lindenwald

In 1977, efforts got underway to restore Martin Van Buren's home to its original glory after Lindenwald had become known as "overgrown, muddy and deteriorating." Between 1977 and 1982, the National Park Service along with conservation contractors commenced with restoration and the organization of its contents and collections. The year 1982 was the bicentennial of Van Buren's birth, with the Columbia County Historical Society establishing many celebratory events, such as an August evening ball under a tent with 400 guests in period attire. In January 1984, the Friends of Lindenwald was established. The goal of this nonprofit organization is stimulating ongoing interest in Pres. Martin Van Buren's history as a politician and farmer. The preservation of his home, Lindenwald, is of high importance, along with the heritage and history associated with it. There are year-round educational programs promoting art and history of the site and opportunities to enjoy the Martin Van Buren Nature Trails. Van Buren was the first American president to be born a citizen of the United States rather than a British subject.

The portrait at left of Martin Van Buren, who lived from 1782 until 1862, is by artist Henry Inman (1801–1846). This painting at the Metropolitan Museum of Art was gifted by the State Historical Society of Colorado in 1949. Van Buren served as a state senator in 1821, a US senator, secretary of state, ambassador to the Court of St. James, vice president, and eighth president of the United States. This Martin Van Buren portrait below was taken by C.M. Bell and published between 1873 and 1916. It was a gift of the American Genetic Association in 1975.

Pictured above is a southeast elevation view at Lindenwald, home of Martin Van Buren from 1839 to 1862, at 1013 Old Post Road, Kinderhook, New York. The image was photographed by Nelson E. Baldwin on January 16, 1937. Colonial Revival architectural elements at the Martin Van Buren National Historic Site include the gatehouse at Lindenwald. The house was formerly known as the Peter Van Ness's Kleinrood house. Van Ness was also known as Petrus Van Ness. Lindenwald is where Washington Irving wrote most of his book *A History of New York*.

A monument to Lindenwald builder Peter Van Ness is shown here. Lindenwald was also once owned by Van Buren's longtime childhood friend William Van Ness. Nelson E. Baldwin took this photograph on January 16, 1937. *The Sentinel* announced two days before Van Buren's March 4, 1837, inauguration, "The citizens of Kinderhook are requested to meet at Stranahan's hotel this evening at half past six to adopt measures for the celebration of the 4th of March, on which day Kinderhook gives a President to the United States."

This image shows the main entrance on the northeast side of Lindenwald. Martin Van Buren resided on the 220-acre farm for the last 21 years of his life before succumbing to complications of asthma during the Civil War. The Friends of Lindenwald were successful in raising money to donate a life-size statue of Van Buren, which was placed next to the bandstand on the Kinderhook Village Green. The statue was dedicated on July 14, 2007. Martin Van Buren Trails are paths through white pine, maple, elm, and birch forests. The author's friend and colleague Daniel J. Gelles has written and directed a short humorous film with Ranger Andrew demonstrating the former president's iconic coffeemaker, a balance syphon, and how it works. The artifact from Europe is over 150 years old and is among the many treasures at Lindenwald.

This image shows the exterior of Lindenwald (listed in the National Register of Historic Places) with trees and shadows. This Lindenwald interior features a mural. Former Kinderhook resident and member of the Friends of Lindenwald Christopher Kline created *O.K.–The Musical* based on history and folklore of his former hometown, and successfully took his production to Tate Liverpool Gallery in April 2017. Kline's musical is about the tracing of Kinderhook's history back to the beginning of the world, the formation of its landscape 4.5 billion years ago, and the first human settlement in the area 12,000–13,000 years ago, with references to Mohican and other Algonquin creation and migratory stories.

A Lindenwald interior that is known as the Green Room includes a harp, and it was here that Martin Van Buren's family and friends would socialize after the evening meal. Many animated celebrations and conversations must have occurred here. Celebrities and politicians of the day were entertained here as well, due to Lindenwald's proximity to both Albany, a day's travel, and Manhattan. In this room, the day's current events would be caught up on along with music and parlor games played and literature read aloud to one and all. The warm environment was undoubtedly where lives were enriched.

These Lindenwald interiors feature one of the more decorative arches used, and a mural. Edward Augustus Collier wrote, "The election of Mr. Van Buren to the Presidency was celebrated in Kinderhook by his townsmen on Saturday the 4th of March with great éclat. At sunrise the National Standard, that victorious, was raised aloft and floated proudly in the breeze. At 12 p.m., a salute of 26 guns (one for each State) was fired, accompanied by the ringing of all bells in the village. At sunset a salute of 12 guns was fired, the bells ringing a merry peal."

These Lindenwald interiors include a dresser and a sitting room. The wife of Pres. Van Buren's eldest son, Abraham, Angelica Van Buren, when recovering from health issues in 1843, was quoted as writing to her mother about one of Lindenwald's pieces of furniture: "I am still chained to my sofa by using great caution I was able to be carried down & laid on the Hall sofa. Lindenwald is a beautiful historic home where it's tempting for its visitors to try out the furniture but must refrain from doing so."

Lindenwald interiors pictured here include a fireplace with portraits in the formal parlor and an ogee in the office. Lindenwald is 20 miles south of Albany and two miles south of Kinderhook village. The site carries on the preservation of the 36-room home of Martin Van Buren. Van Buren's estate became a working farm and he a gentleman farmer in his retirement after his one term as the nation's eighth president. Kitchen vegetables, flowers, grapes, hay, apples, potatoes, oats, and rye were grown on the property.

These Lindenwald interior views showcase the office with desks and bookcases along with the library containing a bust. Becoming known as the "Red Fox" of Kinderhook, the president campaigned for two more terms from rooms at Lindenwald. There was a time lapse of nearly 100 years between the last Van Buren owning Lindenwald and the National Park Service owning it. There were times when Lindenwald was used as nursing home, a restaurant, and an antiques center.

These Lindenwald interior scenes show a beautiful, shuttered office window. Lindenwald's indoor flush toilet, lavatory, and tub were added at the instruction of Martin Van Buren's son Smith, who arrived with his wife to live at Lindenwald; the number of rooms then doubled to 36. In the summer of 2018, the royally appointed mayor of Buren, Jan de Boer, visited Lindenwald and the Luykas Van Alen House. Buren, the Netherlands, is the sister city of Kinderhook. "For my own, I started a few years ago, research, and writing a book, about the relationship of Cornelius Maessen to Martin Van Buren here in Kinderhook, in America, and last year, I got a letter from Mayor Dunham from the village of Kinderhook, and he wanted to investigate the possibilities of a relationship between Buren and Kinderhook," de Boer said. "I said, 'One and one is two. We're going to take that opportunity, and we're going to investigate what we can do.' "

One of Lindenwald's bathrooms features a fireplace and a modern convenience at the time, an indoor flush toilet. Its 1849 installation was for the children's governess, and the room was located close to the children's nursery. The closet is private, with plastered walls and a window. The seat is wood, with a butt-hinge for lifting, and includes a stone-lined well. Toilet paper appeared on the market in 1857.

Images of Lindenwald's bedrooms show sumptuous furnishings. Period sleigh beds are found upstairs and are dedicated to President Van Buren's 11 grandchildren. It is not certain who actually used this room.

Lindenwald's serene looking, pale cream-colored painted kitchen includes the washing up area in the house's cellar, made bright by numerous windows as shown at right. The kitchen cook made daily use of a coal-burning stove and running water. Here is where grand meals were prepared for Van Buren's family and visiting dignitaries, sometimes as many as 20 at one time. It is easy to imagine the smells and hustle and bustle of this important room, central to the functioning and comfort of the estate. It is also where the estate staff, such as farmhands and all servants, had their meals prepared.

Lindenwald was run by the estate's many servants, and the laundry area was run by a laundress. The family clothing and all table linens as well as any other textiles needed to be properly cared for on a daily basis. This room would have been small and hot, and the use of a hand pump generated the water needed to wash clothing. Much labor and long hours would have been expended for these tasks to be carried out. It is important to remember the people who must have toiled greatly to run the estate, mainly refugees from Ireland's "Potato Famine" years.

Martin Van Buren's wife, Hannah Hoes Van Buren, died from tuberculosis in 1819 after 12 years of marriage and motherhood. She never saw Van Buren become president or Lindenwald with its splendors. She was a childhood friend of Martin Van Buren's, but little is known of her. He never remarried, remaining one of few presidents not to have a wife while in office. She was born March 1783 in Kinderhook, with her ancestors having immigrated from Holland in the 1600s. Hannah and Martin were closely related, as their ancestry was intertwined through the small community of early Kinderhook. Hannah Van Buren was related also to the Roosevelts through her mother's ancestral line. Angelica Singleton was married to Martin Van Buren's son Abraham. Angelica acted as hostess during Van Buren's administration. She was instrumental in setting up housekeeping at the Lindenwald estate.

The stair tower at Lindenwald is felt to be symbolic of Martin Van Buren's life, as he was born at the nation's inception and worked toward uniting the country in the years before the Civil War. The staircase connects all additions that were made in 1849 and also connects the old with the new at the Lindenwald estate.

Three

Jesse Merwin, Ichabod Crane, and Washington Irving

Kinderhook is where America's first published ghost story, "The Legend of Sleepy Hollow," with the iconic Headless Horseman, started to form in the mind of author Washington Irving. "Sleepy Hollow" main character Ichabod Crane, the schoolteacher from Connecticut, was based on Irving's close Kinderhook friend Jesse Merwin, a teacher from Connecticut living in Kinderhook in 1808. The Headless Horseman was created during this time and became a terrifying symbol of fear known the world over, giving this region and the Hudson Valley virtual ownership over Halloween. A letter from one important source exists certifying that Jesse Merwin was the prototype for Ichabod Crane. That letter came from former president Martin Van Buren: "This is to certify that I have known J. Merwin of Kinderhook for about 3d of a century & believe him to be a man of honour and integrity; and that he is the same person celebrated in the writing of the Hon. Washington Irving under the character of Ichabod Crane in his famous Legend of Sleepy Hollow."

Another former Kinderhook resident, Harold Van Santvoord, wrote an article in 1898 for the *New York Times* with his point of view. Santvoord had known Jesse Merwin's sons, who shared their family's history with him. While referring to Jesse Merwin as Ichabod Crane, Van Santvoord stated, "I have taken great pains to look up the Merwin genealogy [*sic*], and through courtesy of a son of Ichabod Crane, still living here and highly esteemed for his uprightness of character, have had access to a printed record tracing back this family of English and Welsh extraction on American soil to 1645, when the original immigrant became the owner of a large tract of land lying mostly in the town of New Milford Connecticut. Descendants of Ichabod asseverate that after migrating from Milford, Connecticut, he lived here continuously in Kinderhook."

It is fascinating to think about these real and imagined characters known the world over having their place then, and now, in Kinderhook, New York.

Jesse Merwin, who lived from 1782 to 1852, was Kinderhook's first schoolteacher, having taught at what became known as the Ichabod Crane Schoolhouse, now owned by the Columbia County Historical Society. Merwin's initials are carved into the wood there. The similarities of Merwin's courtship details with a local Kinderhook woman to that of characters courting in "The Legend of Sleepy Hollow" may have been the inspiration Washington Irving drew upon from his friend Jesse Merwin. The author himself at one time addressed a letter to Merwin as "the original Ichabod Crane." Katrina being courted by Ichabod Crane is a popular image re-created in various artistic mediums. (Left, courtesy Edward Augustus Collier's *A History of Old Kinderhook from Aboriginal Days to the Present Time*; below, courtesy Wikimedia Commons.)

Text on this postcard reads, "Among the mannekins of the Columbia County Historical Society, Inc. are Catherine DeGrote Tompkins at the inauguration of Governor Daniel B. Tompkins in 1807, Helen Van Allen of Kinderhook as Katrina Van Tassell in Washington Irving's *Sketchbook*, and Washington Irving who made Jesse Merwin famous as Ichabod Crane in his sketchbook."

This 1907 postcard depicts the famous Ichabod Crane Schoolhouse built by Judge Van Ness, owned by the Columbia County Historical Society. Jesse Merwin, Kinderhook's first schoolteacher, taught here. The land had been in the Van Alen family since its purchase from Mohican Wattawit. Ichabod Crane, Brom Bones, and Dirk Schuyler were based on well-known Kinderhook inhabitants. Katrina Van Tassell is based on Adam Van Alen's daughter Katrina. *Courtship in Sleepy Hollow, Ichabod Crane and Katrina Van Tassel, 1868*, modeled by John Rogers (1829–1904), was gifted by Samuel V. Hoffman to the New-York Historical Society in 1926. It is interpreted by some as possible in the story that Katrina pretends interest in Ichabod to make her other suitor, Brom Bones, jealous and to force a marriage proposal from Brom. (Above, author's collection; below, courtesy Wikimedia Commons.)

The Katrina Van Tassell house, in real life known as the Adam Van Alen House in the Kinderhook Creek vicinity of Kinderhook, was originally built in 1737. A Martin Van Buren letter certifies the connection between Ichabod Crane and Kinderhook resident and friend Jesse Merwin. It is noted by Edward Augustus Collier in his 1914 *A History of Old Kinderhook from Aboriginal Days to the Present Time* that Harold Van Santvoord produced an endorsement of the connection by Washington Irving himself, also in a private letter. Van Santvoord was a writer for the *New York Times* and also the *Albany Times Union* and a descendant through his mother's side of Peter Van Schaack.

The Van Alen Homestead, Where Katrina Van Tassel Lived (1736), Kinderhook, N. Y.

The vintage postcard above depicts the Katrina Van Tassell home in "The Legend of Sleepy Hollow." The image below depicts fall festivities and Halloween decorations. In the story, at a harvest party at the Van Tassells', both Brom Bones and Ichabod Crane vie for the affection and proposal of Katrina. In olden times in Kinderhook, its inhabitants gathered on cold nights near fires roasting apples and told one another of superstitions, ghost stories, and tales of haunted fields in what Washington Irving called "this spell bound region." (Above, author's collection; below, courtesy New York Public Library.)

This portrait is of Washington Irving. He and Jesse Merwin spent pleasant times fishing at Merwin's Lake, beyond the Ichabod Crane Schoolhouse. In 1854, Irving had visited Martin Van Buren after his term as president had ended. The writer had come to Lindenwald 50 years earlier as a tutor to the Judge William Van Ness children at the start of his career in literature. Confirmed in their lifetime by Martin Van Buren, Harold Van Santvoord, and Dr. Bond, editor of the *Christian Advocate and Journal*, Jesse Merwin was the prototype for the character of Ichabod Crane. Many have debated ever since who all the characters were based on in "The Legend of Sleepy Hollow" as well as the location of Sleepy Hollow itself.

These images show homes of Washington Irving: Sunnyside in Tarrytown, New York, and the other his home in New York City. Born in New York City, Irving had the chance as a small boy to meet George Washington, of whom he later wrote an extensive biography. Irving was considered America's first great writer, achieving vast success here and abroad, making his living solely from his craft. An intriguing character himself, Irving came to the Kinderhook area after the death of his love interest Matilda Hoffman; and it was here that the seeds of the paranormal romance "The Legend of Sleepy Hollow" were sown. Also the author of "Rip Van Winkle," Irving crafted characters known the world over, with long-term appeal and charm.

Washington Irving's home Sunnyside is in Tarrytown, New York, where the author retired and lived up to his passing. The Hudson River is visible from the house. Sunnyside is maintained by Historic Hudson Valley, and tours of the house are available that feature its original furnishings and pop culture artifacts related to "The Legend of Sleepy Hollow" story, first published in 1820, as well as artwork inspired by the story. Nearby in October is the Great Jack O'Lantern Blaze, in Croton-on-Hudson, New York, the biggest lighted pumpkin festival in the tristate area. The characters created in Irving's story have inspired advertising and art since their creation.

Merwin Farmhouse was owned by Jesse Merwin after time boarding at Judge William Peter Van Ness's house. At the judge's home, Merwin and Washington Irving met; Irving was also a boarder there. Merwin died in Kinderhook November 8, 1852, after marrying Jane Van Dyke and having eight sons and three daughters. Tarrytown Cemetery is shown here as well, sometime between 1860 and 1930. The Merwin Farmhouse was reputed to be haunted by subsequent owners. While 1940s actress Esther Tuttle is on record as having no experiences herself, she had been told in great detail about some of the otherworldly events happening to her family at the farmhouse.

Jesse Merwin's tomb rests in the Kinderhook Cemetery. Martin Van Buren's letter attests to the fact that Jesse Merwin, close friend of author Washington Irving, was the prototype for the character Ichabod Crane in "The Legend of Sleepy Hollow." Known by many at the time, the identities of Irving's characters seemed to have been lost to time and became a topic of debate among scholars. *The Headless Horseman Pursuing Ichabod Crane*, an 1858 painting, is by John Quidor and one of the most recognizable images of this theme. In "The Legend of Sleepy Hollow," Irving writes, "In the dark shadow of the grove, he beheld something huge, misshapen, black and towering. It stirred not, but seemed gathered up in the gloom, like some gigantic monster ready to spring upon the traveler."

At left, the Adam Van Alen House, built in 1737 and located on Route 9H in Kinderhook, is believed to be the house that the home of Katrina Van Tassell in "The Legend of Sleepy Hollow" is based upon, where the fall harvest takes place preceding the dramatic conclusion of the ghost story. The home is a National Historic Landmark and open to tours seasonally. The image below is of Washington Irving Church in Tarrytown, New York. It was published by the Detroit Publishing Company in 1901. The ivy growing on the church was taken from cuttings from Washington Irving's home, Sunnyside. His pew remains in the front of the sanctuary.

The Dutch Reformed Church in Kinderhook organized in 1712 was the sixth church between Albany and New York City; before its inception, spiritual services were offered from Albany. The churchyard contains the grave of Martin Van Buren. The first Reformed church was built in 1677, the second in 1717. The third church was built in 1814 at the site of the present church and was badly damaged by fire in 1867. Rebuilt in 1869, it stands at its present location on the corner of Church and Broad Streets in Kinderhook. It offers an Open House Celebration with Kinderhook's Village Candlelight Night. Scholars debate the original inspiration for the Old Dutch Church in "The Legend of Sleepy Hollow."

Images here show the Old Dutch Church and the Headless Horseman Bridge in Tarrytown, New York. The church is located on Route 9—also known as the Queens Road, after Queen Anne— and Albany Post Road, which in olden times was used to deliver mail from New York City to Albany on the east side of the Hudson River. It was originally a Native American trail from Manhattan Island and became a main road when the Dutch arrived.

Two images portray townsfolk of Sleepy Hollow, now a village 25 miles north of New York City. In olden times, it was a misty place full of superstitions and folklore. Sleepy Hollow, according to some, had contained the bridge where the chase between Ichabod and the Headless Horseman culminated in Ichabod being blasted by a pumpkin. The wooden bridge spanning across the Pocantico River was most likely lost to time through decomposition. Sleepy Hollow historians can document at least five different bridges that held this function: carrying the Albany Post Road over the river now replaced by US Route 9. As Irving writes, "The bridge became more than ever an object of superstitious awe, and that may be the reason why the road has been altered of late years, so as to approach the church by the border of the millpond."

A view of Sleepy Hollow (left) and a Currier and Ives print of Sunnyside, Washington Irving's home in Tarrytown, New York, (below) are shown here.
The Old Dutch Church and its burying ground from 1685 are suggested by some to be locations in Irving's story: "Indeed, certain of the most authentic historians of those parts, who have been careful in collecting and collating the floating facts concerning this spectre, allege that the body of the trooper, having been buried in the church-yard, the ghost rides forth to the scene of battle in nightly quest of his head; and that the rushing speed with which he sometimes passes along the Hollow, like a midnight blast, is owing to his being belated, and in a hurry to get back to the church-yard before daybreak."

A beloved symbol of the fall harvest season is the pumpkin—one of which was discovered and blasted at the last known place Ichabod galloped through. An element of debate and interest in "The Legend of Sleepy Hollow" was the question of whether the Hessian soldier's head or a pumpkin instead had been hurled at Ichabod during the ghostly gallop. Pictured at right, the real Col. Ichabod Crane (1787–1857) reportedly was not happy—bordering on being mortified—that his name was used for a character in Washington Irving's tale. Irving and the colonel met in 1814 at Fort Pike on Lake Ontario.

The image above is identified as the Van Tassell house, later bought by Washington Irving, Esq., to refurbish as a summer home; Irving would later name it Sunnyside. The Old Dutch Church, Sleepy Hollow, in Tarrytown, New York, is shown below; it is a 1904 print from the Detroit Photographic Company. After losing a significant local business in the 1990s, the Village of North Tarrytown changed its name to Village of Sleepy Hollow, subsequently capitalizing on the fame of Washington Irving's story. In the tale, the Old Dutch burying ground is where the chase between Ichabod and the Headless Horseman was to end, with the phantom disappearing.

Four

ARCHITECTURE

One of the best sources for local architecture is *A Visible Heritage: Columbia County, New York: A History in Art and Architecture* by Ruth Piwonka and Roderic Blackburn, which offers far more information and images than can be brought here. Piwonka, village historian, and Blackburn are both longtime members of the Kinderhook Historic Preservation Commission.

Within Kinderhook, the commission strives to preserve the integrity of the village's properties, protecting the architectural integrity long-term for residents and visitors. Many of Kinderhook's early majestic homes were built with bricks baked in Holland and imported to this country. Records from 1661 show bricks imported from Holland and sold for $4.18 per thousand, while also there were at least two brickyards known to be operating in early Kinderhook. Soil near the river is mostly clay, great for brickmaking. Early brickyards were in existence on Eykebush Road (now spelled Eichybush) and on the Schermerhorn-Pruyn and Van Alstyne farms as well. Pine was also used in early home building.

Collier's *A History of Old Kinderhook from Aboriginal Days to the Present Time* reports of the A.T. Ogden House (above): "Mr. Levi Milham built in 1858, and occupied until his death is shown here. This thrifty farmer's family were a memorable household. Mr. Alfred T. Ogden purchaser of the Milham estate, very greatly beautified it, has made the house and grounds among the most attractive in this whole region." The Benedict Arnold Inn (below) has also been known as the Chrysler House. Collier says, "The late Thomas Beekman reported Arnold, months after wounded in the battle of Bemis Height, borne through Kinderhook on a stretcher and passed a night at this inn; and that the door-way being too narrow to admit the stretcher, one of the jambs was temporarily cut away. The house was built, according to date on southend, in 1770, and the site was a part of the original Pruyn estate."

"Flying Stairway" in the Entrance Hall of Columbia County's House of History, Kinderhook, N. Y.

The Van Vleck house, later the Bank of Kinderhook's location from 1859 to present, is shown in an 1816 postcard printed in Williamsville, Massachusetts. A handwritten message reads, "I am visiting here now. Best regards." The postcard was sent to a Mr. John Roth in Troy, New York. Organized in October 1808, the Kinderhook Conscript Society was formed with Adam Van Vleck elected as treasurer. Abraham Van Vleck was one of the incorporators of the 108 Chatham Turnpike from Stuyvesant to Chatham. Flying Stairway, at the James Vanderpoel House of History, is shown here in a 1940s postcard. Regional folklore exists from the building's past employees' reports of it being haunted.

Pictured above is a Tuck's Oilette postcard, printed in England, depicting Lindenwald; the back reads, "Raphael Tuck and Sons, Art Publishers to their Majesties the King and Queen." The greeting card and postcard business started in the 1800s in London, but Tuck and Sons never fully recovered after German bombing against Britain in 1940 and 1941 destroyed the firm's headquarters, Raphael House. Oilette refers to the type of printing method used. An exterior view of the James Vanderpoel House of History is shown below. Vanderpoel was also the builder of what was known as the Burt House.

House of History of the Columbia County Historical Society, Inc., located at Kinderhook, N.Y.

The above fireplace detail is from Martin Van Buren's home Lindenwald. After 1848, Van Buren retired there permanently. The Spencer Hinds house was photographed by the Library of Congress in 1933 as part of its Historic American Buildings Survey (HABS). Few changes have been made to Kinderhook Village, allowing it to retain its old charm and historic character. In 1974, it was listed in the National Register of Historic Places. Kinderhook's architecture includes features that are Federal, Greek Revival, and Carpenter Gothic in style.

The above view of the Spencer Hinds house was published by the Library of Congress in 1933 as part of the HABS. A Lindenwald door detail is demonstrated at left. Lindenwald offers free tours, both in person and virtual tours through its website, so visitors may learn about "the Red Fox of Kinderhook."

The Abram or Abraham Staats House is believed to be the oldest in the region and was constructed in 1664 with three-foot-thick walls and is located near the Columbiaville Bridge and nearby train tracks in Stockport. It was burned by Indians then rebuilt. Staats's original tenant was killed, with his wife being carried off by Indians believed to be from Canada. Staats purchased 200 acres along Stockport Creek from Mohicans in 1654; he then leased his "bouwery, house, barn and rick" to Jan Anderissen, who was known as John the Irishman. The house is standing today on Station Road and recently sold for over a million dollars. Stockport was originally included in the Powell and Kinderhook grants made to Major Staats in 1667. Edward Augustus Collier writes, "A neck of land called by the Indian name Chickhakwick lying and being on the East side of the River Striking along the great Kill to the first Great Fall of water and from thence to the fishing place where there is a tree mark't with the letter A."

Above is a view of the Staats house, believed to be the oldest in the county, and the image at left shows a large earthen pot discovered in the home's cellar. It is believed to be a grain or possibly wine jar. These images appear in Augustus Collier's *A History of Old Kinderhook from Aboriginal Days to the Present Time*, published in 1914. Collier, along with his colleague William Wait, documented much of Kinderhook's early history in images and text by visiting area residents as well as state offices in Albany. In the era before the Internet and of slower travel methods, it is truly impressive at how much information they garnered. Collier notes that upon meeting Wait in the local cemetery around 1907, Wait suggested that the two men take on this history endeavor. Generations ever since are grateful to them for doing so.

Five

NOTABLE RESIDENTS PAST AND PRESENT

Past and present times in Kinderhook, New York, have attracted an impressive array of visitors and residents. Music, television, and movies have been inspired and filmed on location here. *Sister Kinderhook*, music by Rasputina, was inspired by the Dutch architectural elements in the village.

A character from the television show *The Sopranos* owned a farm first mentioned in the episode "All Due Respect," and it was apparently located at 146 Route 9A in Kinderhook; it is mentioned in multiple episodes, including the season five finale. Tony Soprano's cousin, murdered at this location, describes being called Ichabod Crane as a teenager who had been visiting the farm. Daniel Day-Lewis and Michelle Pfeiffer spent time here filming scenes for *The Age of Innocence* at the Luykas Van Alen house. Bradley Cooper and Robert De Niro, in their 2012 film *Silver Linings Playbook*, discuss the origins the expression "OK" and Kinderhook over dinner. As a director, Mary Stuart Masterson, known for her role in the 1986 film *At Close Range*, with Sean Penn and Christopher Walken, chose Kinderhook to film scenes from her 2006 film *The Cake Eaters*. One of the most fascinating people ever, Harry Houdini filmed one of his movies in Valatie Village. And Kinderhook is now the home of The School, Jack Shainman's internationally known art gallery.

Sidney Poitier's children attended school in Kinderhook. Weighing less than three pounds at birth, Poitier was not expected to live. Son of a Bahamian tomato farmer, Poitier left his homeland for America and went on to become the first African American Hollywood leading man. The star of numerous films, he won the Academy Award for Best Actor for the 1963 film *Lilies of the Field*. Known to be an extremely private person, Poitier wrote a memoir, survived an almost fatal car accident, and directed Richard Pryor's last film. Poitier said, "I was imbued with my idyllic life in the Caribbean, where there was sunshine and turtles and birds and no white people. It never occurred to me that I couldn't come to America and do whatever I wanted to do. Naive as that was, it was a blessing."

Martin H. Glynn was a Kinderhook resident and governor of New York State (1913–1914). He is shown here in a Harris & Ewing photograph. Born in the town of Kinderhook on September 27, 1871, Glynn lived in the village of Valatie until December 14, 1924. Of Irish descent, he graduated from Fordham University, then studied law at Albany Law School. On December 15, 1924, his *New York Times* obituary read, "Former Governor Martin H. Glynn died in his home here today. Mr. Glynn returned yesterday from a hospital in the suburbs of Boston, where he had been under treatment during the last two months for spinal trouble of long standing. Members of his family said he complained last night of not feeling well." The real cause of his death—suicide—was exposed in Valatie historian Dominick Lizzi's 1994 biography *Governor Martin H. Glynn: Forgotten Hero*. Glynn was the first Irish American, Roman Catholic head of government.

The former Martin Van Buren School is now home to an internationally known Jack Shainman 30,000-square-foot art gallery. The School, at 25 Broad Street, Kinderhook, is open to the public on Saturdays. This 1948 postcard back reads "Hi there Al: We are in the state of New York tonight staying at Seneca Falls. I miss the gang from the station. Say hello to all of them for me. Joe M. Machado." The former Martin Van Buren School served students as an elementary and high school and closed in 2012. Recently, The School held an exhibit of Harold Van Santvoord's prints from a 19th-century limerick book containing portraits of then Kinderhook residents. The book had been donated to the Kinderhook library in the 1990s by the Van Schaack family but was lost to time and then found again in the Kinderhook Library.

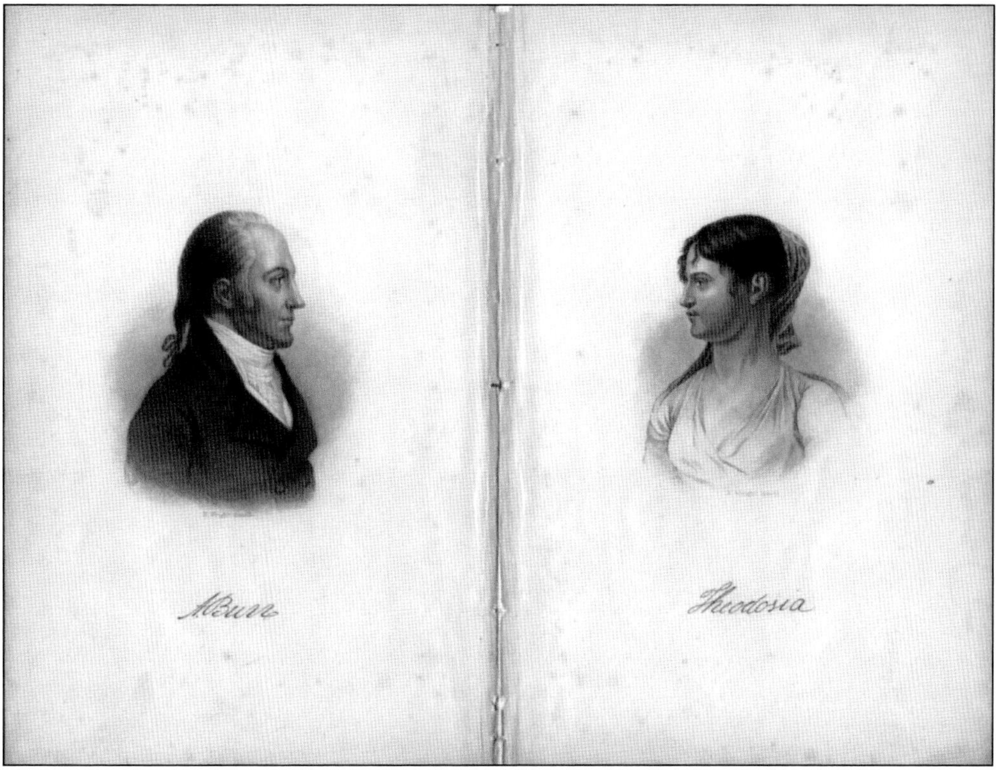

Aaron Burr, second vice president of the United States, is pictured above with his daughter Theodosia. A son of Peter Van Ness, William P. Van Ness was Aaron Burr's friend and as such communicated Burr's challenge to Alexander Hamilton and acted as his second at the 1804 duel that ended Hamilton's life with a gunshot. According to local legends, William Van Ness gave Aaron Burr hideout in a secret, sealed room at Lindenwald after Burr's killing of Hamilton. At right is a portrait of Alexander Hamilton by artist John Trumbull. Hamilton lived from 1757 to 1804.

The legendary beauty of the dark-haired Jenny Jerome, Lady Jenny Spencer Churchill, is demonstrated here in two 1921 images of former British prime minister Winston Churchill's mother. Of his mother, Churchill wrote, "She shone for me like the evening star. I loved her dearly—but at a distance." A British socialite who worked as a magazine editor, she was born in Brooklyn. She lived in Kinderhook after her father, New York financier Lawrence Jerome, acquired Lindenwald when it was lost by Martin Van Buren's son John due to a gambling debt. Famous for her attractiveness, she was described as having "more of the panther than of the woman in her look" by Lord d'Abernon. The Churchills and Spencers have been related since the 1700s, with the two most prominent figures in recent times being Sir Winston Churchill and Lady Diana Spencer, later Diana, Princess of Wales.

Harry Houdini filmed *Haldane of the Secret Service* in 1923 in the village of Valatie near Beaver Kill Falls. Houdini had first made a name for himself in the 1890s, capturing the public's fascination by being an escape artist. One of his feats was to be chained to a wooden crate then tossed into New York's East River. The public gasped, but Houdini always managed to escape. Houdini died on Halloween 1926. During life, he became obsessed with the afterlife when his mother passed away. He began contacting psychics and mediums to attempt communication with his beloved mother, only to be continually disheartened when learning of their parlor tricks and the type of stage magic that he knew all too well from his own performances. After tirelessly engaging in the debunking of the spiritualists and mediums of his day, Houdini vowed that if there was a way to communicate from the Great Beyond—that he would. The Houdini Motion Picture Company made many silent films, depicting his escapes, which remain unexplainable to this day.

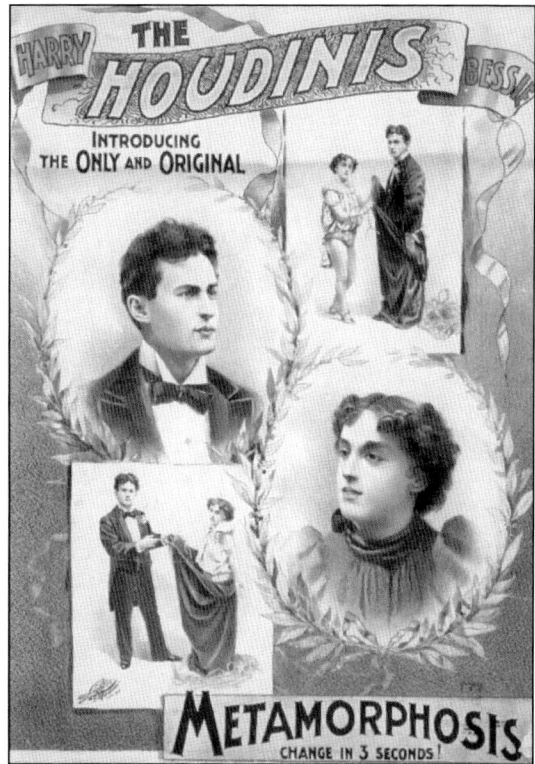

Edith Wharton's novel *The Age of Innocence* created excitement again during the 1990s when Martin Scorsese's film adaptation of the novel was filmed at the Van Alen House, Kinderhook. Wharton, who lived from January 24, 1862, to August 11, 1937, was a celebrated American novelist and short story writer who was the first woman to receive the Pulitzer Prize for Literature, in 1921. She wrote about the American aristocracy and values and morals of the 19th century. The expression "keeping up with the Joneses" was said to be about her father's family, as her birth name was Edith Newbold Jones.

Six

FOLKLORE AND LOCAL LORE

With Kinderhook's long history, links to the American Revolution, and melding of different ethnic groups and immigrants, it's only natural that some folklore, mythology and local legends would have been passed down from the area's early days to the present time. Some of the local architecture is said to retain energy from the past, and Kinderhook has many of its own early period ghost stories. In her memoir, Esther Tuttle, an actress during the 1940s, describes the letter in her possession that was written by Pres. Martin Van Buren confirming that Jesse Merwin was the original prototype for Ichabod Crane. Merwin married Jane Van Dyck, and they had 11 children. Jesse and Jane are buried in Old Kinderhook Cemetery, also known locally as the Dutch Reformed Cemetery.

THE following are the Names of the Persons proposed to be elected as a COMMITTEE on *Tuesday* next, agreeable to the Recommendation of the CONGRESS. New-York, Nov. 17, 1774.

Isaac Low,
Philip Livingston,
James Duane,
John Alsop,
John Jay,
Peter Van B. Livingston,
Isaac Sears,
David Johnston,
Charles Nicoll,
Alexander M'Dougall,
Thomas Randall,
Leonard Lispenard,
Edward Laight,
William Walton,
John Broome,
Joseph Hallet,
Charles Shaw,
Nicholas Hoffman,
Abraham Walton,
Peter Van Schaack,
Henry Remsen,
Peter T. Curtenius,
Abraham Brasher,
Abraham P. Lott,
Abraham Duryee,
Joseph Bull,
Francis Lewis,
John Lasher,
John Roome,
Joseph Totten,

Thomas Ivers,
Hercules Mulligan,
John Anthony,
Francis Basset,
Victor Bicker,
John White,
Theophilus Anthony,
William Goforth,
William Denning,
Isaac Roosevelt,
Jacob Van Voorhees,
Jeremiah Platt,
William Ustick,
Comfort Sands,
Robert Benson,
William W. Gilbert,
John Berrian,
Gabriel W. Ludlow,
Nicholas Roosevelt,
Edward Flemming,
Lawrence Embree,
Samuel Jones,
John De Lancey,
Frederick Jay,
William W. Ludlow,
John B. Moore,
George Januwa,
Rodolphus Ritzma,
Lindley Murray,
Lancaster Burling.

The Van Schaack mansion was built in 1774 of brick baked in Holland kilns and imported to the New World by David Van Schaack. Edward Collier writes, "After his voluntary exile in England during the Revolutionary war, his brother, Peter Van Schaack, the distinguished jurist and friend of John Jay, lived there for a while, and when totally blind taught an advanced law class in his garden on the premises adjoining. General Montgomery on his way to Saratoga, and General Burgoyne when a prisoner of war, were entertained there by the Van Schaacks, and also Aaron Burr, John Jay, and the famous Chancellor Kent, author of that stupendous work in thirty volumes, 'Commentaries on American Laws.' "

Apples being checked after harvesting in Kinderhook were said to be "OK," and that is one explanation for the origin of the expression. During the presidential election of 1840, it was used as an expression and that it is the oldest written reference to it, since Martin Van Buren had been nicknamed "Old Kinderhook." It is quite possibly an abbreviation of "orl korrect," a humorous form of "all correct" used commonly at the time.

Gordon Wilmot, in a book published by J. Merone & Company, wrote, "There is a story of a young girl treated terribly; the history of Rosina Jones, a cottage maid, who suffered from poverty and cold, cast out from her father's home to which is added a distinct and vivid statement of Stephen Dorsey, her betrayer and the murderer of her child, perpetrated in the woods near Kinderhook, N.Y. : also containing a glowing account of the pathetic interview with her father who refusing her shelter, she was frozen to death beside the cottage door on the night of the dreadful snow storm, February 20th 1854."

A 1909 postcard depicts Hendrik Hudson and was published by Jerome H. Pemick & Co.; this image is from the collection of Vivian Yess Wadlin. According to journals of the time, Henry Hudson entertained some Mohicans aboard his ship the *Half Moon*. Fur trading with Mohicans began a year after Hudson's departure back to his home in the Netherlands. Subsequently, the Dutch came up the Hudson River every summer for furs. Author Shirley Dunn wrote of a symbolic, but reassuring gesture in which "the natives broke their arrows and threw them into the fire so Hudson would not be afraid." The Mohicans were a strong and numerous tribe at the time of Hudson's arrival in 1609 and for about 20 years afterward. Mohican land extended from Vermont to Manhattan, including lands on both sides of the river. (Courtesy Hudson River Valley Institute.)

In 1941, the actress Esther Tuttle and her husband bought the Merwin farmhouse. In her 90s, Tuttle was interviewed as having said that she herself never experienced anything but that her family had several encounters with an apparition or ghost on the porch. She said that the door to the bedroom where her mother-in-law usually stayed would unlock and open repeatedly. Her mother-in-law described hearing the thumb latch on the door lift many times and that she would be wide awake while hearing this. Esther's grandson described a "white mommy" on the porch, which frightened him. Tuttle later had elderly descendants of the Merwins' visit and explain that their sister often slept on the porch to ease her ailments and that she died in that location in 1917.

The attic at Lindenwald is purportedly one of the rooms that may be haunted there, and speculation that Aaron Burr's spirit lingers has been noted in several books, including *Empire Ghosts: New York State's Haunted Landmarks* by Lynda Lee Macken, *Haunted Presidents: Ghosts in the Lives of the Chief Executives* by Charles A. Stansfield, *Haunted Hudson Valley: Ghosts and Strange Phenomena of New York's Sleepy Hollow Country* by Cheri Farnsworth, and *Ghost Investigator: Hauntings of the Hudson Valley*, volume 1 by Linda Zimmermann. Legend has it also that the spirit wanderings of Martin Van Buren himself, along with that of his favorite son, John, have been seen in the dining room.

ROBT. MC WADE
AS
RIP VAN WINKLE.

While Washington Irving enjoyed Kinderhook, he was known to also have created the character and story of Rip Van Winkle. Tom Illari, of Catskill Collectibles, says, "2018 will celebrate the anniversary of the most prominent resident of the Catskills who actually never resided there. Rip Van Winkle. It was in June 1818 that Washington Irving penned the classic short story. Rip Van Winkle itself is widely thought to have been based on Johann Karl Christophe Nachtigal's German folktale "Peter Klaus." This story, set in a German village, tells of a goat herder by the name of Peter who goes looking for a lost goat. Peter finds some men drinking in the woods and after drinking some of their wine he falls asleep. When he wakes back up, twenty years have passed." The 1787 Rip Van Winkle House was the oldest house in the Catskills.

Pentecost was one of the main universally celebrated Dutch colonial holidays. Virginia O'Hanlon, shown here in 1895, was the little girl who at eight years old wrote to *The Sun* newspaper: "Dear Editor, I am 8 years old. Some of my little friends say there is no Santa Claus. Papa says, 'If you see it in The Sun, it's so.' Please tell me the truth, is there a Santa Claus?" She received a reply forever famously known as "Yes Virginia, There Is a Santa Claus." This literature has become a part of annual Christmastime celebrations ever since its initial publication. Virginia spent her final days at the Barnwell Nursing Home in Valatie and passed away at 81 after living in North Chatham for many years. The North Chatham Historical Society honors Virginia at Christmas by reading her letter and Church's beautiful reply at her gravesite in the North Chatham Cemetery.

Santa Claus and St. Nicholas have been used interchangeably to invoke images of the Christmas season. Early Dutch settlers of Kinderhook would have resisted celebrations connected to a Catholic observance, but centuries later, the two characters figured prominently in Hudson Valley holidays. In the 1600s, Christmastime for the Dutch would have been two days of church services and fasting. The Dutch did cite Saint Nicholas when traversing the uncertainty and dangers of the seas while traveling. Sinter Klaas and images of him adorning ships were believed to offer protection and good luck. The Bronck Museum in Coxsackie, Greene County, devoted to early Dutch history, offers a St. Nicholas Day during its "Chilly Willy Winter's Eve" weekend but has asserted that there is no evidence of this type of celebration being recognized in the early Dutch colony of New Netherland.

Seven
A Mosaic of Kinderhook

In the time and space provided in this book, one hopes to capture what Kinderhook was and is. Its imagery, folklore, architectural elements, and literary culture as well as contributions to the nation's history deserve preserving. Photographs were at times hard to track down, and many important to Kinderhook's history are too compromised to republish. The Columbia County Historical Society in Kinderhook is a treat to visit, with many artifacts and images as well as a library and gift shop where regional history books can be used for research and/or purchased. In this chapter, the reader sees images concerning Dutch and Indian times, the American Revolution, the nation's presidents, suffragettes who fought for the right to vote, examples of Kinderhook's architecture, major motion pictures filmed in Kinderhook, famous historical sites, Kinderhook's connection to the nation's first written ghost story, Kinderhook's first families, and its early means of commerce.

This 1914 Valatie postcard was printed in Germany by the P.S. Dresden Company. The Santa Claus Club in Valatie was created in 1944 by 15 men of the area with their army separation to provide a holiday and gifts for the poor. It was the first in the nation to be created after area clothing mills had ceased operation and employment ended for many locals. A parade started at 3:30 p.m. in the village followed by a visit from Santa with gifts to children 10 and under in their homes. The Valatie Post Office seasonally places a Santa's Mailbox for children to send their letters to Santa. Founders of the club include Bill Farrell, Bob Kelly, and Wally Brough. Jane Merrifield remembers, "This is the Santa Group I remember. . . . I was one of the 1st bunch of kids that they came to. I lived on Main St. in the Stucco building that has since been torn down . . . and I had never seen Santa . . . heard about him."

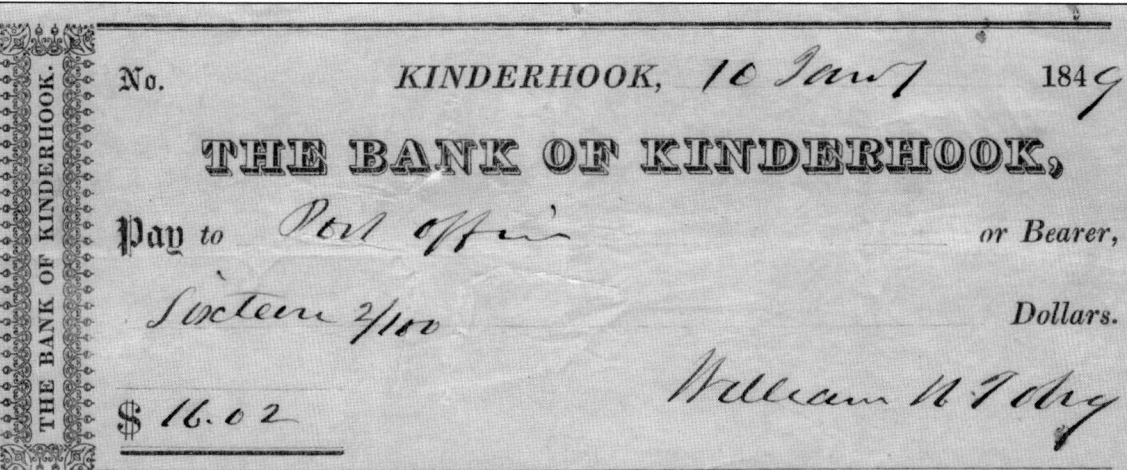

A January 10, 1849, Bank of Kinderhook check is shown here made out to "Post Office" for $16.02. Edward Collier states, "As early as 1826 and several times thereafter, attempts were made to establish a bank at Kinderhook, but without success until October 9, 1838, when subscribers to a capital of $113,525 met at Stranahan's hotel, adopted articles of association and elected the first Board of Directors of the Kinderhook Bank. They were: John P. Beekman, John Bain, Uriah Edwards, Teunis Harder, Adam H. Hoysradt, Peter I. Hoes, Lucas Hoes, Mordecai Myers, Edward Pugsley, John I. Pruyn, Adam Van Alstyne, Lawrence Van Buren, David Van Schaack, William H. Tobey, John J. Volkenburgh, Charles Whiting and Julius Wilcoxson. The bank began business in January 1839. The building used was owned by Br. Beekman."

These vintage postcards depict the former amusement park that Kinderhook offered for locals and tourists. Above, two ladies in period clothing and hat walk along the mechanics of an amusement ride. The Electric Park Village near Kinderhook Lake also contained a Waiting Room and Store, depicted in the 1920s postcard below with text on the building that reads as follows: "Risedorph's Soft Drinks, Always Bread and Cakes & Pies Fresh Every morning, Lunches and Branch of Valatie Pharmacy." In 2017, the Columbia County Historical Society held an exhibit showcasing the amusement village and its significance.

A 1910 vintage postcard depicting the Ferris wheel at Kinderhook's Electric Park was published by Frank Dougherty, of Albany, New York. With its main line running between the two cities, the Albany and Hudson Railroad created the park; in 1902, one million passengers road this line. Since the line was not bustling on weekends, the railroad company created the electric park on 40 acres to increase its traffic and revenue.

A September 25, 1780, letter written by Benedict Arnold to George Washington in which Arnold pleads for mercy for his wife produced a response from Washington for the beautiful young wife to have an escort back to her family in Philadelphia. Kinderhook's participation in the Revolutionary War saw some of the war's prominent heroes and traitors passing through here. Originally considered a hero, along with Ethan Allen, for taking Fort Ticonderoga in 1775 and assisting with British general John Burgoyne's surrender at Saratoga in 1777, Arnold later changed loyalties to the British side and led raids in Connecticut and Virginia. A 1770 brick home in Kinderhook, now privately owned, has a plaque outside reading, "According to tradition Benedict Arnold was brought here after being wounded at Battle of Bemis Heights 1777."

Kinderhook and Valatie were first connected by telegraph in December 1861. Sylvester Becker, president of Valatie village, sent the first message to Kinderhook president W.H. Tobey: "Our two villages are connected by telegraph wires. May we ever live in friendship and brotherly love, ever assisting each other as opportunity offers." The reply from Kinderhook was, "Kinderhook reciprocates the greeting of Valatie, and while she follows in the track of her improvement acknowledges with motherly pride the daughter's progress and prosperity." (Guglielmo Marconi later invented the wireless telegraph.) Kinderhook's first newspaper was the *Kinderhook Herald*, created in 1825 by Peter Van Schaack, whom Collier describes this way: "the proprietor and editor was a well-educated scholarly man of excellent literary ability and refinement."

The Hudson River and smaller waterways were used by the Dutch for transporting goods. The river was originally called the Mohicanituk, or "Grandmother," by the Mohicans, Kinderhook's first inhabitants. The river was a constant resource for Mohican daily life. Yearly flooding of the Hudson created rich soil for their agriculture, and shellfish were plentiful. The Hudson-Fulton Celebration in 1909 marked the 300-year anniversary of Henry Hudson's exploration of the river. "Taconic" is a Mohican word, and thousands of the tribesmen lived in the valley at the time of the Dutch foreigners' first visit. Mohican numbers would decline after foreign settlement due to factors such as introduction of diseases they had no resistance to.

Robert Livingston was an immigrant from Ancram, Scotland, and bought thousands of acres from the Mohicans. He owned a total of 160,240 acres and was one of the nation's Founding Fathers as well as one of five men who drafted the Declaration of Independence. He was made lord of Livingston Manor. In 1710, he sold 6,000 acres of his property to Britain's Queen Anne for use as work camps and resettlement of refugees from Germany. Clermont Manor, built in 1728 in the town of Clermont, was the home of Livingstons for over six generations. In 1765, Hendrick Claue entered into an indenture with Robert Livingston Jr. for land in Kinderhook written at Manor of Livingston, New York. Robert Livingston Jr. agreed to lease a house, barn, and orchard in Kinderhook to Hendrick Claue for one year. In exchange, Claue was expected to pay rent and keep the property in good repair.

In 1993, the Martin Scorsese film adaptation of the Edith Wharton novel *The Age of Innocence*, with events taking place in 1870s New York City, filmed one of its scenes at the 1737 Dutch colonial Luykas Van Alen House in Kinderhook. Michelle Pfeiffer, Daniel Day-Lewis, and Winona Ryder star in the film, with some Pfeiffer and Day-Lewis scenes taking place at the historic site. Scenes filmed mostly in Troy depict early Manhattan. The movie lushly illustrates longing and the bittersweet life of someone marrying the wrong person. Of the film, Vincent Canby of the *New York Times* wrote, "Taking *The Age of Innocence*, Edith Wharton's sad and elegantly funny novel about New York's highest society in the 1870s, Martin Scorsese has made a gorgeously uncharacteristic Scorsese film. . . . The film is the work of one of America's handful of master craftsmen."

A rendering of an Indian village is depicted here and was originally published in the 1914 Edward Augustus Collier book *A History of Old Kinderhook from Aboriginal Days to the Present Time.* Collier lived from 1835 until 1920 and was a Congregational minister at Kinderhook, New York, and author of "Thou, Lord, art God alone" (Holy Trinity) in the *Scotch Church Hymnary* of 1898.

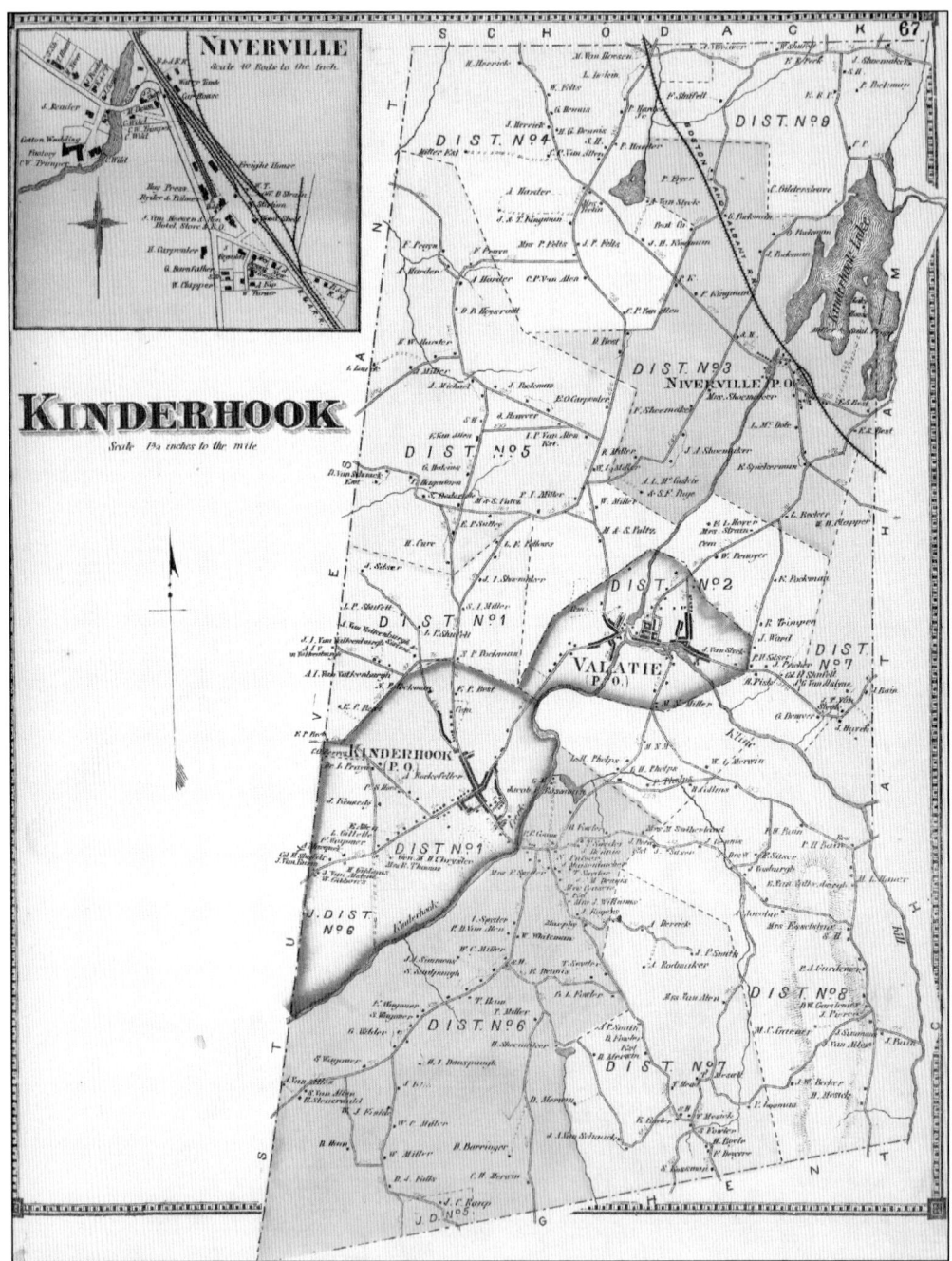

Pictured is an early map depicting Kinderhook with Niverville and Valatie, "Niverville Village, Kinderhook Township." The image is from the Lionel Pincus and Princess Firyal Map Division of the New York Public Library Digital Collections, 1833. Early Kinderhook was Niverville, North Chatham, Chatham Center, Valatie, Ghent, Stockport, and Stuyvesant. (Courtesy New York Public Library.)

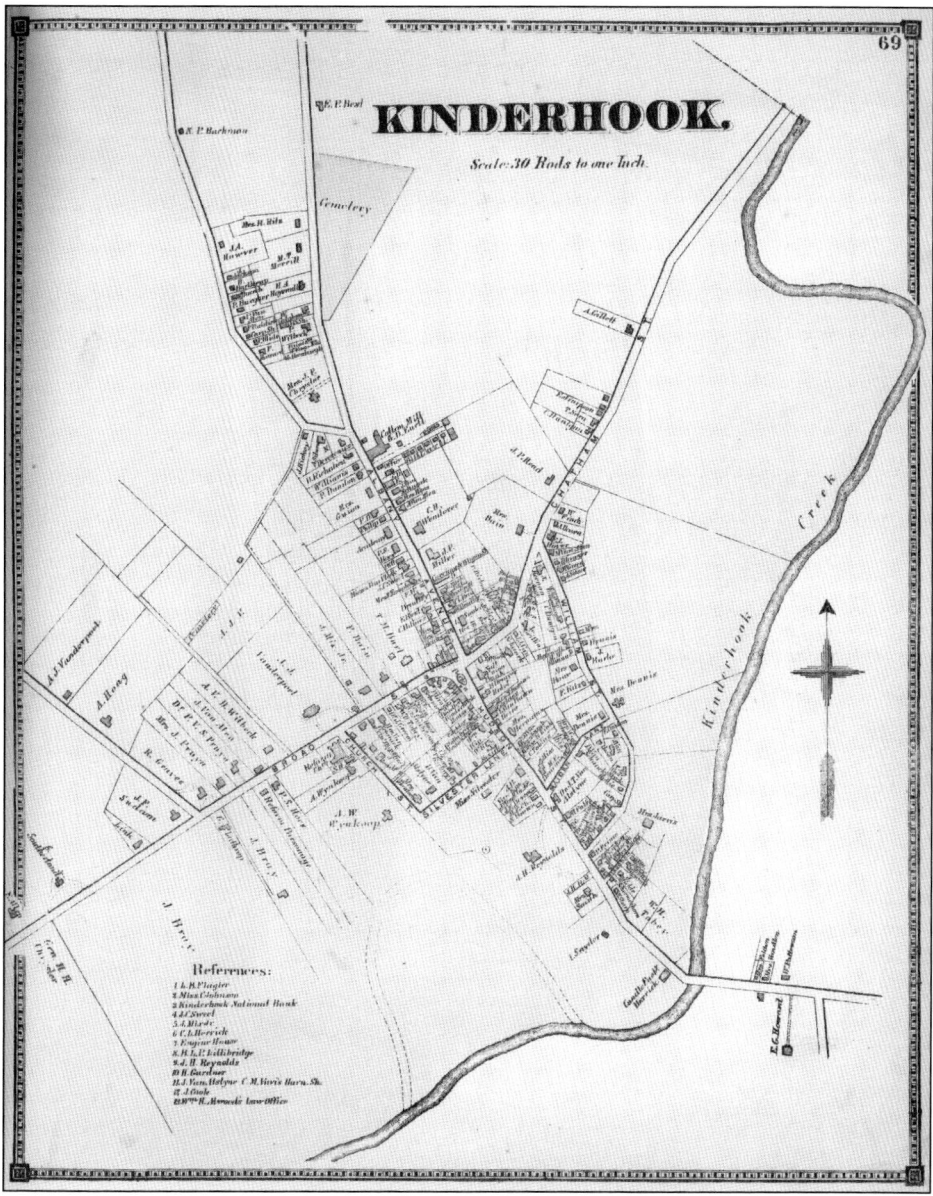

An early map depicting Kinderhook village shows a cotton mill. The image is from the Lionel Pincus and Princess Firyal Map Division, at the New York Public Library, 1833. "A History of Kinderhook, NY (Part 1)" in H.P. Smith's *Columbia County at the End of the Century*, printed by the Record Printing and Publishing Co., Hudson, New York, 1900, states, "The manufacture of hats was once an important industry here, Rodolphus Graves having a factory near the Reformed church." The blog *Upstate Earth* notes, "When the first Dutch settlers came to this corner of Columbia County in New York State around 1650, they took advantage of the ample water power to establish mills for the grinding of grain and production of lumber. In the early 1800s, the Industrial Revolution initiated in New England came here when the English-born Nathan Wild built cotton mills on the Valatie and Kinderhook Creeks. These early mills and factories directly transferred the energy generated by falling water to looms and other machinery." (Courtesy New York Public Library.)

MARTIN VAN BUREN

1837 **Eight President of the United States** 1841

Born—Dec. 5, 1782, Kinderhook, N. Y.
Died—July 24, 1862

Wm. T. Lawley,
53 Beverly Ave.,
E. Lansdowne, Pa.

Martin Van Buren, the eighth president of the United States, was born and is buried at Kinderhook. He is attributed with coining the term "OK." According to local historians of New York State, this originally stood for "Old Kinderhook." This expression has become known and used the world over. Van Buren's ghost supposedly haunts his old home of Lindenwald, although many are not prone to encouraging this folklore. Lindenwald still stands just off Route 9H, not far from the original Ichabod Crane Schoolhouse. This postcard was mailed from Kinderhook in 1934 and describes Martin Van Buren as the "eight" president of the United States; it is in the collection of the author.

An 1840 White House portrait of Martin Van Buren's beautiful daughter-in-law Angelica Singleton, who was related to Dolley Madison, was painted by Henry Inman. Madison was instrumental in introducing Angelica to Martin Van Buren at his inaugural ball. Singleton grew up on a South Carolina plantation owned by her wealthy father. She lived with her husband, Abraham Van Buren, at Lindenwald and spent winters in South Carolina. Singleton acted as White House hostess since Van Buren was a widower, was given the title of first lady, and was the youngest woman to hold that distinction. After travel to Europe, Angelica decided to bring some of its style to both the White House and Lindenwald.

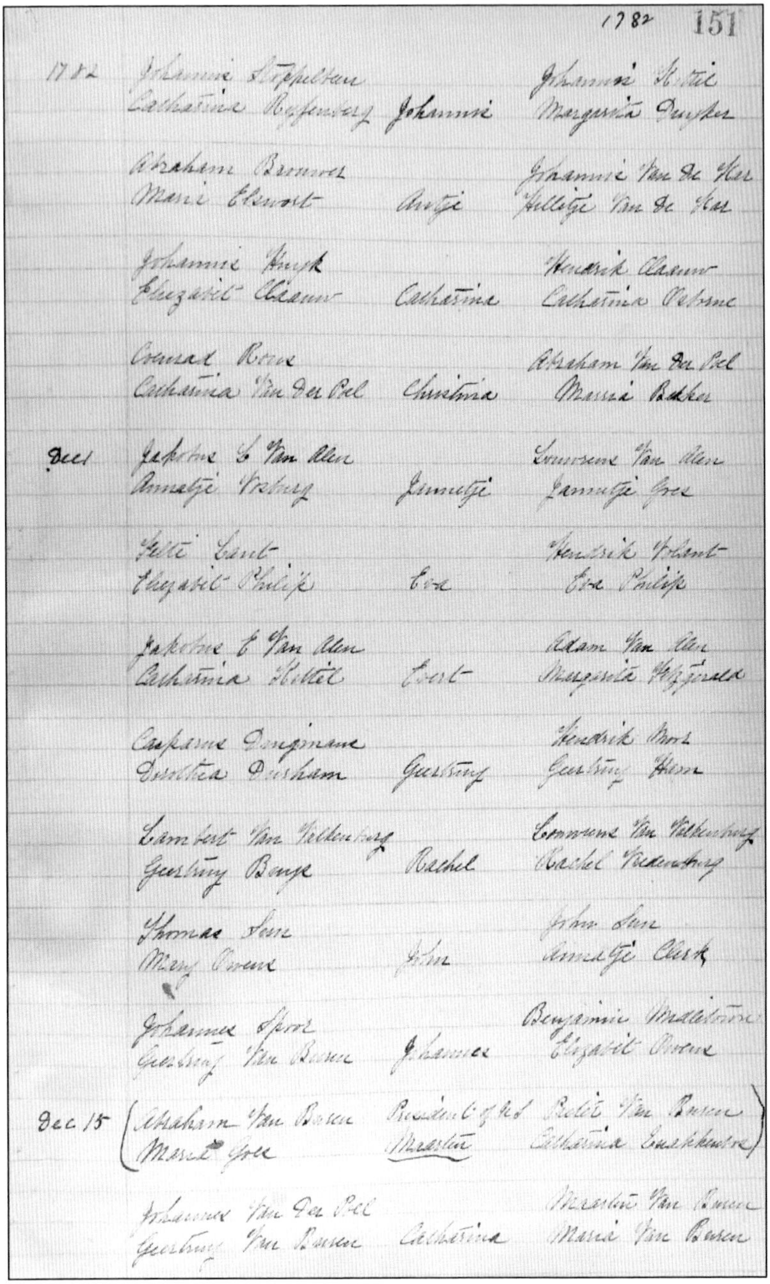

This image shows Martin Van Buren's baptism record; the page is from baptism records at Kinderhook, New York, Dutch Reformed Church. Van Buren was baptized on December 15, 1782. In "A History of Kinderhook, NY (Part 1)," Van Buren is described as such: "After returning from abroad Mr. Van Buren led a quiet and domestic life at Lindenwald. He was fond of horseback riding, and could be seen almost every day in the saddle, his silvery locks flowing under a close fitting skull cap[.] When an old man he jumped into the creek one day and rescued his grandson from drowning. Almost every Sunday found him hymn book in hand in an old fashioned, square, high backed pew in the Reformed Dutch church. If the weather was cold it was his custom to cover his bald head with a fur driving glove."

In his journal describing his visit to Kinderhook, Henry Hudson writes, "I sailed to the shore in one of their canoes with an old man, who was the chief of a tribe consisting of 40 men and 17 women; these I saw there in a house well constructed of oak-bark, and circular in shape, so that it had the appearance of being built with an arched roof. It contained a great quantity of maize . . . and beans of the last year's growth, and there lay near the house for the purpose of drying enough to load three ships, besides what was growing in the fields." Hudson noted that Kinderhook's fertile land was the best for cultivation that he had ever seen or set foot upon.

An oil on canvas painting of an unknown date by artist John Frederick Kensett, who lived from 1816 to 1872, is in the private collection of a Kinderhook resident. *Tree in a Landscape* is 17.9 by 24 inches. Kensett was a member of the second generation of the Hudson River School of artists; the school was not an actual school as such but rather a group of like-minded artists who started America's first art movement, originating in Hudson and the Catskills. This movement dominated American art for most of 50 years, though later on drawing criticism for being "too literal and grandiose." Thomas Cole is known to be the founder of the Hudson River School, whose painting subjects were the surroundings landscapes. Kensett was one of the founders of the Metropolitan Museum of Art.

> Manor Livingston 16 Jan'y: 07
>
> Dear Sir
>
> The Bearer hereof one Philip Adam Chenbragh one of our Tenants (and man of good Charector) is gott into some trouble concerning a Negro fellow he bought some time before last in the last Disturbances. I have recomended him to you to manage his Cause for him agt. his Antagonest please to examine him and do the best his Cause will admitt for him. He is an industrous honest man and think his case hard and should be sorry he should suffer —
>
> Yr Very Hhbl Svt
>
> Peter R. Livingston.

Edward Collier states, "In later days many others prominent in social and political life received a cordial welcome in this historical home, the list of invited guests including Henry Clay, Washington Irving, Thomas H. Benton, David Wilmot, Silas Wright, Azariah C. Flagg, William L. Marcy, Francis P. Blair, Commodore Nicholson, and the Earl of Carlisle. On Henry Clay's visit, the year previous to his death, he dined in the same room in which the captive British general had been entertained three quarters of a century before. When Dr. John P. Beekman succeeded to the property it was a favorite resort of Martin Van Buren and his Lindenwald guests. The Van Schaack house is now, and has been for many years, the summer residence of Mrs. Aaron J. Vanderpoel, a granddaughter of Peter Van Schaack."

This painting depicts Ichabod Crane courting Katrina Van Tassell; both characters were based on early Kinderhook residents. Katrina's character represents conflict for the protagonist and antagonist both vying for her hand in marriage. Descriptions of her imply fertility and a strong-willed, wily woman who knows what she's doing. "The Legend of Sleepy Hollow," listed by the Library of Congress as one of the Books That Shaped America, was written by Washington Irving in his collection of essays and short stories titled *The Sketch Book of Geoffrey Crayon, Gent.* About the character Ichabod Crane, "The Legend of Sleepy Hollow" notes, "He would have passed a pleasant life of it, in despite of the Devil and all his works, if his path had not been crossed by a being that causes more perplexity to mortal man than to ghosts, goblins, and the whole race of witches put together, and that was a woman."

The National Union Bank of Kinderhook was located in the Lathrop Building in 1853, before moving in 1859 to the Van Vleck House, where it is located today. Kinderhook Bank opened for business on October 1, 1853. Dori McDannold states, "The banking facility is believed to have been located in the north end of the frame building that housed Lathrop and Reynolds Hardware store in Kinderhook, New York. The building was leased from Gen. Charles Whiting and stood on the southwest corner of Broad Street and Albany Avenue. On December 28, 1858, bank president William H. Tobey purchased the Van Vleck property for $5,250. The bank occupied the property on May 1, 1859. The first president of the bank was William H. Tobey, the first vice-president was John Bain, and the cashier was William H. Rainey. At the time of the organization of the bank, the nearest banks outside the village of Kinderhook were those in Albany to the north, Pittsfield to the east, Hudson to the south, and Coxsackie to the west." (Courtesy Dori McDannold, Kinderhook Bank.)

From Collier's *A History of Old Kinderhook from Aboriginal Days to the Present Time:* "The bank continued business without special incident until the great panic of 1857, which placed a severe strain on the financial institutions of the time. In the following year, on the 15th of September, the bank was robbed by burglars, who succeeded in blowing open the outer and inner safes with powder and securing about ninety-five hundred dollars in cash, which the bank subsequently recovered. Immediately after the robbery, the bank purchased the premises on the corner of Chatham and Hudson Streets and proceeded to fit up the brick building thereon for the use of the bank, constructing a very substantial vault of the then best-known materials, with the best doors and inner safes that could then be procured. The bank occupied this building in the spring of 1859."

Peter Stuyvesant, also known as Petrus or Pieter, was the last Dutch director general of the colony of New Netherland until 1664, when it was then renamed New York. Stuyvesant and Stuyvesant Falls are named after him, as are neighborhoods and apartment complexes near New York City. Juanita Knott, a Stuyvesant, New York, historian, states, "Stuyvesant is in the northwest corner of Columbia County, bordered on the north by Rensselaer County, the east by the Town of Kinderhook, the south by Stockport and the west by the Hudson River. Archaeological evidence demonstrates the Native Americans were in partnership with the land along the river's edge long before Henry Hudson made his exploration in 1609. They fished the river, planted corn and pumpkin. Communication was probably carried out by signal fires built on the shale hill above the waters they named Muhheakunnuk, meaning 'great waters or sea— constantly ebbing and flowing.' "

PETER STUYVESANT
From a painting from life, in the possession of the New York Historical Society

1. Peter Stuyvesant defying the English who demanded the surrender of New Amsterdam 1664, a few days later Stuyvesant was forced to submit. (Scale Model)

Museum of the City of New York
5th Ave. & 104th Street

The author of *The Age of Innocence*, Edith Wharton lived here at her home called The Mount. It is located in Lenox, Massachusetts. Although she was never known to have been to Kinderhook, her novel was adapted for film by Martin Scorsese and partially filmed in Kinderhook, at the Luykas Van Alen House, among other Upstate New York locations. Wharton designed The Mount herself, and it was built in 1902 on a property of over 40 acres. Subsequently, the house was used as a boardinghouse for girls and the site of a private theater company, Shakespeare & Co. The Mount now offers tours, such as a Backstairs Tour and a Ghost Tour. The Syfy series *Ghost Hunters* filmed an episode there after many years and reports of paranormal activity. The Mount is near Tanglewood and the Norman Rockwell Museum and partners with over 40 other cultural organizations to offer many events for visitors.

An early 1940s postcard depicts Rainbow's End, a restaurant and rooming house that was located on what is now Route 9 in Valatie. An ad in the July 9, 1955, *Troy Record* reads (typos and all), "Relax and Enjoy on Hour or Two at Rainbow's End VALATIE, N. Y. A well-known spot for years / Under the personal supervision of a well-known culinary connoisseur of the Capital District. With prices to fit the purse strings of any family AND FOOD! to satisfy the palate of a gourmet Catering to Parties, Weddings and Banquets / For reservations call Murdock 4-9831."

Edward Collier states, "The wolves infesting the forests were so numerous and became so bold in their slaughter of sheep and cattle that in 1726 a bounty was offered here, as had long been done in other parts of the Colony, for their destruction. The bounty for the killings of a full-grown wolf was in the first instance six shillings, less for one under one year of age. In a few years this was increased to 10, then 12 shillings. For some unknown reason unless it was the superior adeptness

of the Indians their bounty was but half that allowed a white man. The head of a wolf and the entire skin were to be taken before a Justice and the ears cut off in his presence as a protection against fraud. Later in 1775 the bounty amounted to three pounds." (Albert Newsam lithograph, courtesy of the Library of Congress.)

This October 1941 photograph is of the train station in Chatham, completed in 1875 and photographed by John Collier Jr. (1913–1992) for the Library of Congress as part of the Farm Security Administration – Office of War Information Photograph Collection. Kinderhook Bank opened in October 1853; at the time, the only other banks in the region were in Albany and Pittsfield. Kinderhook Bank purchased the train station building in 1990 to be used as its Chatham branch. A "great panic" of 1857 put severe stresses on the financial institutions locally. Collier writes that in September 1858, the Kinderhook Bank was robbed "by burglars, who succeeded in blowing open the outer and inner safes with powder and securing about ninety-five hundred dollars in cash, which the bank subsequently recovered. In March of 1865, the bank was converted into a National bank under the Laws of the United States, under the title of the National Union Bank of Kinderhook, and continued, as provided by law, for twenty years until 1885, when its corporate existence was extended for another twenty years, until 1905."

Until about 1810, there were a number of slaves in the town. This 1941 image is of the Chatham House, operated by J.B. Sinclair and also known as the Chatham Hotel. It was photographed by John Collier Jr. At the time of this writing, Al Roker and Tatum O'Neal have houses in the area.

These vintage postcards show the serene undeveloped farmland of early Chatham. When Wendy Knight of the *New York Times* visited Chatham for an article in 2003, she called Chatham "less gentrified and touristy than Lenox or Great Barrington but slightly more polished than the outposts of the Catskills." Richard Hallock, the Chatham town supervisor, said, "Twenty years ago, there were 20 plus working farms. Today, there are two." The organic Old Chatham Sheepherding Farm makes sheep's milk cheeses and yogurt enjoyed by the likes of Christie Brinkley, and it raises and sells lamb to many New York restaurants. Chatham now enjoys a growing art scene and has become a popular location for second-home owners from New York City, New Jersey, and Connecticut—collectively known as "weekenders."

The Stanwix Hotel in Chatham is where Harry Houdini stayed in 1924 while filming one of his movies, *Haldane of the Secret Service*, costarring Gladys Leslie, Adele Ormsby, and Edward Ormsby. It was filmed at Beaver Kill Falls in Valatie. As a child, Houdini moved with his family to New York City, where Harry became interested in magic. In the 1920s, spiritualism swept through America, and Houdini was intrigued as much as anyone. After continually exposing many spiritualists as frauds, Houdini started receiving death threats and curses thrown at him. In 1894, Houdini had married the love of his life, singer and dancer Beatrice Raymond, or Bess, as he would call her. Between them, they created a code known only to them for Houdini to prove after his death if there was an afterlife. The code would spell out "Rosabelle, believe."

A vintage postcard depicts an aerial view of Chatham. The village was incorporated in 1869, with William Thomas, one of its earliest settlers, owning much of the village and opening its first business, a tavern in the 1811 building. A three-story building known as The Clocktower at the end of Main Street still boasts a working clock. Albert S. Callan, the village historian said on November 25, 1988, that "the Great Fire of 1869 broke out at 2:00 a.m. of April 5 on the west end of Main Street, and, swept by a strong wind, it burned building after building, despite the efforts of Ocean Fire Company No. 1 and its old hand engine. Telegrams were sent to Albany and Hudson for help, and fire apparatus was dispatched to Chatham via railroad cars to help fight the conflagration." Moe Howard of the Three Stooges owned a home in Chatham for many years.

A Stockport wool mill is pictured here in a 1933 Library of Congress image. Stockport was a part of early Kinderhook that was noted for its early manufacturers and its waterpower. Stockport was originally a Mohican village, and it is believed to be at a spot where Henry Hudson may have landed. James Wild's five-story cotton mill was there. Wild, born in Stockport, England, imported raw cotton from slave states, which was then turned into textiles. Ruins of the mill can still be seen from the Route 9 bridge and the Columbiaville gorge. Stockport was an area diverse in mills, with shipping, cloth, paper, and other goods being produced there. Peter Stott's extensively researched book *Looking for Work: Industrial Archeology in Columbia County, New York* is a valuable resource and a necessary addition to a collection of Columbia County history. Ethnological objects from an archaeology dig there exist at the New York State Museum in Albany. Stockport Creek empties into the Hudson River. Fossils of trilobites from the Cambrian period have also been found there.

In 1971, Frank Serpico, a Brooklyn policeman, was shot in the face during a drug bust. After the 1973 Sydney Lumet movie *Serpico*, starring Al Pacino in the title role, Frank Serpico became one of the most loved heroes in film history. The real Frank Serpico lives quietly here in the home he built on the Hudson River, frequenting area libraries and coffee shops to people-watch and visit with friends. He is working on a memoir. In 2015, *Newsweek* reported that Serpico "lost his bid for a seat on the town board of Stuyvesant." He was reported as saying that the loss "probably saved him a big headache." This image shows the Italian poster for the film. (Courtesy Heritage Auctions.)

A dart that was used before the invention of the bow and arrow, from the Late Archaic Period, was appraised by the New York State Museum in Albany and was determined to be 4,000 years old. As professor at the University of Rochester and member of the New York State Archaeological Association, Ken Mynter completed an excavation of an Indian shelter nearby yielding evidence that the site was used 5,000 years ago. Carbon tests proved that cooking fires were used there as far back as 3,000 BC, with remnants of meals eaten there: mussel shells and animal bones were found. In 1984, while writing for the *Independent* (the independent newspaper in Hillsdale, New York), Mynter wrote, "Indians were living here in this county before the building of the pyramids while our own ancestors were living in the New Stone Age in Europe. After spending thousands of years in a vast valley with no one else but their own, it is remarkable that the Mohicans let us in." (Courtesy Lisa LaMonica.)

Donald Shriver, president emeritus of Union Theological Seminary in New York, and Stephen Kent Comer added a historical marker alongside the already-existing History of Columbia County marker at the northernmost overlook of the Taconic Parkway. The original marker tells of Hudson's arrival in 1609, with no mention of the Mohicans. After years of fundraising and work with a variety of state agencies, and with the help of St. Peter's Presbyterian Church in Spencertown, New York, the men decided it was necessary to commemorate the Mohicans who had greeted Hudson and his crew. Around 1736, the Mohicans left this area and New York for Stockbridge, Massachusetts, then settled in Wisconsin, where today their descendants exist as the Stockbridge-Munsee Community, Band of Mohican Indians. Bonney Hartley is the tribal member in Troy now representing Mohicans; she and the author's friend Stephen Kent Comer are enrolled tribal members. Comer noted, "I can say that when I came to this area thirty years ago, I was amazed to find virtually nothing about my people in their native land. It was as though we were a ghost people."

Donald Fisher was the New York state paleontologist from 1955 to 1982, a noted scholar, and maintained the OK Rock Shop on Route 9 in Kinderhook village upon his retirement. From all accounts, Fisher loved maintaining his shop, met with collectors from foreign countries, and gave schoolchildren tours there. His work as such included development of correlation charts for the Cambrian, Ordovician, and Silurian systems of the state. His shop showcased fossils and jewelry and included specimens of Cambrian period trilobites collected in 1947. "The fossil tracks are real. The coelophysis is the only known New York dinosaur – 3m long, 39 kg," as quoted by Robert Pullman, who writes the blog New York Road Trip, after visiting the rock shop and interviewing Fisher. In his 80s, Fisher began the work of authoring the book *The Rise and Fall of the Taconic Mountains: A Geological History of Eastern New York*, published by Black Dome Press in 2006. Fisher died at the age of 90, on Christmas Eve 2012.

A 1910 vintage postcard depicts Kinderhook Lake and the Electric Park. The Kinderhook Lake Corporation was formed in 1953 as a nonprofit entity. A boat parade is held every Fourth of July, and flares are sold to create "a ring of fire" around the lake. Kinderhook Lake was one of the first in New York State to be electrified, with some of the first electric lights and amusement park rides in the country at Electric Park, formerly on the east bank of the lake. People from Boston also traveled here to enjoy the amusements, with the park closing during World War I.

Andrew Jackson and Martin Van Buren were instrumental in the Indian Removal Act, signed into law by Jackson and enforced under Van Buren's presidency. Christopher Kline said, "The US government's policy of ethnic cleansing called 'The Indian Removal Act of 1830' executed by the 8th US President, Kinderhook's own Martin Van Buren, sent them from Stockbridge to a shared Wisconsin reservation. The Munsee Stockbridge community still exists there with a population of 1,565 people, though the last speaker of the Mohican language died in 1933. Today, only one registered Mohican descendant lives in their historic territory of the Hudson River Valley." Some Indians went peacefully, while naturally others strongly resisted.

In October 1777, uniformed American Revolutionary soldiers, under the command of Maj. Gen. Philip Schuyler of Albany, approached the Van Schaack house to take Maj. Gen. John Burgoyne as a prisoner of war and Burgoyne's army to Massachusetts after their defeat at Saratoga. Burgoyne's troops were in a wooded area nearby as he prepared to dine at the Van Schaack mansion. From a ballad of the time, Edward Augustus Collier wrote, "For the bold Burgoyne was marching, With his thousands marching down, To do battle with the people, To do battle for the crown. But Stark he lay at Bennington, By the Hoosic's water's bright, And Arnold and his forces, Gathered thick on Bemis height." Several of Burgoyne's German soldiers were won over by the attractiveness of Kinderhook women and deserted the army to make their permanent homes there.

These images show the "Little Brick House 1770," also known as Benedict Arnold Inn, and an 1894 portrait of Arnold himself; a reproduction of a painting by John Trumbull, copyrighted by Ed Frossard. Arnold's name is synonymous with being a traitor. He first served as a general during the American Revolution, later becoming known as a turncoat and defecting to the British side in 1780. After he was entrusted by George Washington to protect West Point, Arnold's plan was to turn the fortification over to the British, but his scheme was discovered. He was able to escape, while his cohort Maj. John André did not and was subsequently hanged. Arnold and his wife later relocated to England. His motives were most likely due to his indignation at being passed over for promotions by the Continental Congress. The house still stands in Kinderhook village and is a private home no doubt visited by locals and tourists alike. Arnold stayed a night at this house after being wounded in the Battle of Bemis Heights.

Edward Augustus Collier, author of *A History of Old Kinderhook from Aboriginal Days to the Present Time*, is pictured at left. Below is an image of an early Indian village that he wrote about. "Certainly if a tithe of the magnitude and difficulty of the work had been realized, it would never have been undertaken. A short paragraph sometimes represents long and laborious research," Collier was quoted as saying when referencing his book. He and friend William Wait set out to put together a comprehensive history of Kinderhook during olden times and well before the age of the Internet. They traveled extensively to Albany, Hudson, Kingston, and New York City to gather material from sources such as descendants of the Vanderpoels and Van Schaacks.

These 1914 images of Broad Street in winter and the Kinderhook Hotel appear in Edward Collier's *A History of Old Kinderhook from Aboriginal Days to the Present Time*. His 1864 quote is endearing to readers still: "With great trepidation I first set foot in Kinderhook, April 9, 1864, having come from Amenia to Niverville. There was no expectation of ever seeing the place again. Much less was it dreamed that it would be home for more than fifty years, the birthplace of five children, the resting place of the departed, and the one spot in all the world endeared by life's most sacred and tender associations."

Built in 1774 with brick baked in Holland and imported to this country by David Van Schaack, the Van Schaack mansion was fortified against intruding Canadian Indians. But Van Schaack was known for his hospitality to welcome visitors. The Van Schaacks were among the first Kinderhook inhabitants coming from the fur trade in Albany that was established by their ancestors. David and his brother Peter, whose house was next door, both practiced law, as did their father. For a time, both David and Peter were exiled in England during the Revolutionary War but were

afterward allowed back to Kinderhook and their homes. The Van Schaacks were involved with groups opposed to British rule, events and actions precipitating the war. Their grand house entertained Chief Justice John Jay, Alexander Hamilton, Gen. Philip Schuyler and, later, "The Legend of Sleepy Hollow" author, Washington Irving. History happened at this house. Both very grand houses remain on Route 9 in the village of Kinderhook.

The first Santa Claus Club in the nation was started in Valatie in 1946 by 15 local men providing holiday toys to children after clothing mills vital to the area's workers had died out. These 15 men used their army separation pay to prevent a bleak holiday for families. A tradition of Santa's Parade through the village, with the music of "Here Comes Santa Claus" played at 3:30 in the afternoon and Santa himself visiting the homes of children under 10 years old on Christmas Eve began. It has been a thriving annual tradition ever since, with other communities nationwide adopting the practice. That first Christmas Eve, courtesy of the Santa Claus Club, Santa himself visited the homes of the little children.

This image depicts "Mike Clancy and his Kinderhook-Hudson Mail Carrying Outfit" in the 1870s, from an old sketch by Harold Van Santvoord and published in Edward Augustus Collier's *A History of Old Kinderhook from Aboriginal Days to the Present Time*.

This image from 1914 shows the village square of Kinderhook and appears in Collier's book. Harold Van Santvoord was a prolific writer, having started writing—at 15 years old—a weekly comic for a New York publication. He also wrote for the *New York Times* and the *Albany Times Union*, albeit for the *Times Union* he largely wished to remain anonymous. His writing career flourished, and it remained his profession until his death. *Life* magazine was founded in 1883, and Van Santvoord was a valued regular contributor. On January 8, 1913, he was found dead in his chair "with paper and pie in hand."

According to Edward Augustus Collier, "These are 1914 images of the Pruyn-Bray-Beekman homestead and the Parsonage of the Reformed Dutch Church at Eykebush Road from a brook crossed by a bridge down to the Kinderhook Creek, north of the land of Stephen Van Alen. The lots on which now stand twelve or more of the nearest buildings on Broad Street were within its bounds, as were also the lowlands down to and including the present residence of Mr. Davie. The Misses Catharine and Maria Pruyn, Miss Anna H. Wilcoxson, and the heirs of the late Captain Bartholomew Pruyn are owners to this day of portions of their great-great-grandfather's original estate. Cornelius Schermerhorn is spoken of as a blacksmith. As Arent Pruyn, who succeeded him ,also had a blacksmith shop, it seems probable that *both* dwelling and shop had been built by Schermerhorn before 1736. Arent Pruyn's wife, Catryna Gansevoort, was closely related to the Conyns, already residing in the vicinity, and that is supposed to have influenced the coming here of the first of the Pruyns. They were both communicant members of the Dutch church here in 1736."

Elmhurst and Crow Hill are shown here in 1914 images from Edward Collier's *A History of Old Kinderhook from Aboriginal Days to the Present Time*. The first owner of Elmhurst was Judge Julius Wilcoxson, who used it as his summer home. The house was originally owned by the Van Alens and was eventually sold to Gen. Charles Whiting, who also owned Crow Hill. James Vanderpoel owned Crow Hill, and Mohican chief Wattawit was the property's first landowner. The property once had a fishpond, until local legend has it that all fish were killed after a lightning strike. General Whiting, a stove merchant, purchased the property to make a grand home for his wife, Margaret Rogers. This property is listed in the National Register of Historic Places. Crow Hill is featured in the June 2018 issue of *Hudson Valley Magazine*, where it was offered for sale for $2.7 million.

These headstones reside in the Persons of Color Cemetery, on Rothermel Avenue, Kinderhook, New York, and listed in the National Register of Historic Places. Established in 1861 by John Rogers for Kinderhook's enslaved residents after their passing, the cemetery was continually used until all available land was filled. Rogers was from Ireland and moved to Kinderhook in 1795; he later resided in the Van Schaack house until his death in 1815. (Courtesy William Krattinger.)

Charles E. Van Volkenburg died in 1849 before reaching the age of two. His headstone is also found in the Persons of Color Cemetery on Rothermel Avenue. The inscription reads, "Sleep sweet babe, thou art at rest, not a cloud of sorrows is shaded o'er thy breast; thou was fair and lovely as thy budding rose, sleep child of beauty, sweet is thy repose." At the time of the 1790 census, Kinderhook and Claverack had the most slaves within New York State. Any black person born in New York State after 1799 was free. (Courtesy William Krattinger.)

This is a Library of Congress image of 26-year-old Henry Knox, who, as the Continental Army's artillery commander, received orders from George Washington, November 16, 1776, regarding the British Invasion of New York: "You are immediately to examine into the state of the Artillery of this army & take an account of the Cannon, Mortars, Shels, Lead & ammunition that are wanting; When you have done that, you are to proceed in the most expeditious manner to New York; There apply to the president of the provincial Congress, and learn of him, whether Col. Reed did any thing, or left any orders—respecting these things, & Get him to procure such of them as can possibly be had there. The president if he can, will have them immediately sent hither; If he cannot, you must put them in a proper Channel for being Transported to this Camp with dispatch before you leave New York. After you have procured as many of these Necessaries as you can there, you must go to Major General Schuyler & Get the remainder from Ticonderoga, Crown point, or St. Johns—If it should be necessary, from Quebec, if in our hands—the want of them is so great, that no trouble or expence must be spared to obtain them—I have wrote to General Schuyler, he will give every necessary assistance, that they may be had & forwarded to this place with the utmost dispatch—I have given you a Warrant to the paymaster General of the Continental army, for a Thousand Dollars, to defray the expence attending your Journey, & procuring these Articles, an Account of which you are to keep & render upon your return. Given under my Hand at Head Quarters at Cambridge this 16 day of November Annoque Domini 1775."

DISCOVER THOUSANDS OF LOCAL HISTORY BOOKS
FEATURING MILLIONS OF VINTAGE IMAGES

Arcadia Publishing, the leading local history publisher in the United States, is committed to making history accessible and meaningful through publishing books that celebrate and preserve the heritage of America's people and places.

Find more books like this at
www.arcadiapublishing.com

Search for your hometown history, your old stomping grounds, and even your favorite sports team.

Consistent with our mission to preserve history on a local level, this book was printed in South Carolina on American-made paper and manufactured entirely in the United States. Products carrying the accredited Forest Stewardship Council (FSC) label are printed on 100 percent FSC-certified paper.